DINNER TIME
CONVERSATIONS

DINNER TIME CONVERSATIONS

8 PRINCIPLES FOR RAISING CONFIDENT, INDEPENDENT, AND FUTUREPROOF KIDS

RICK KETTNER

Copyright © 2025 by Richard Kettner. All rights reserved. No part of this book may be used or reproduced in any manner whatsoever without written permission except in the case of brief quotations embodied in critical articles and reviews.

The information provided in this book is for informational purposes only and is not meant to be a substitute for professional advice.

Kettner Media Inc.

paperback ISBN - 978-1-0696842-0-2
e-book ISBN - 978-1-0696842-1-9
audiobook ISBN - 978-1-0696842-2-6

Contents

Introduction		1
PRINCIPLE 1	Support Kids' Growth with a Daily Routine	11
PRINCIPLE 2	Nurture Kids' Curiosity Through Self-Selected Hobbies	21
PRINCIPLE 3	Build Flexible Knowledge Through Diverse Experience	41
PRINCIPLE 4	Shape Positive Behaviors with Effective Modeling	53
PRINCIPLE 5	Nurture Problem Solving with Open-Ended Questions	71
PRINCIPLE 6	Reinforce Kids' Growth with Detailed Praise	87
PRINCIPLE 7	Boost Skill Development with Proven Strategies	105
PRINCIPLE 8	Cultivate Happiness Through Positive Reflection	121
Conclusion		139
Acknowledgments		145
Notes		147
Works Cited		151

Introduction

When I was sixteen years old, I dropped out of high school to become an entrepreneur.

It was 1998, in the midst of the dot-com boom. The internet was just starting to explode in popularity, and I had been spending my free time building simple websites and studying what was then cutting-edge technology. It was a period of rapid innovation, and I was learning everything I could about the latest advancements in the tech world.

Unfortunately for me, as excited as I was to turn my enthusiasm into a career, I still had nearly two years of high school to complete before I could graduate.

One day, I mentioned to my father how frustrated I was to be stuck in school while so many amazing things were happening all around me. It felt like I was missing out on a once-in-a-lifetime opportunity to ride the wave of innovation that was building momentum at that very moment. Unexpectedly, he asked if I had considered leaving school early.

This blew my mind.

I had never thought of that as a possibility, despite the fact that both my father and his father had left school early, my father in eleventh grade and my grandfather in sixth. Things were different when they grew up, it seemed to me. Not as many people went to college, and white-collar jobs didn't yet make up such a large part of the workforce. But I was growing up in the '90s, the era of television PSAs warning teens against pregnancy, cigarettes, *and* dropping out of school.

After the shock of my father's question wore off, I became determined to make it happen.

Fast-forward some twenty-five years. There has been no shortage of challenges, but over this time period I've built and sold three successful businesses in online music education. As a result, work has become optional in my life. I'm still involved in many interesting and fulfilling projects, but earning an income is no longer the necessity it was in the past.

Now to be clear, I'm *not* recommending that you encourage your children to leave school. That's *not* the message of this book. I only share my unique story because it recently inspired me to reflect on *why* the choice I made was ever offered to me. I wondered what it was that caused my father to conclude I could be successful without finishing school or earning a formal degree.

Furthermore, I wanted to understand how *three consecutive generations of high school dropouts*—my grandfather, my father, and I—had gone on to achieve financially successful, rewarding lives. And we had done so during a period of technological change unprecedented in human history.

More importantly, I wanted to know if there was a recipe for raising my own three kids to thrive in an increasingly unpredictable world. And if so, could it be distilled into a set of clear, actionable principles that any parent could use to create a brighter future for their children?

After extensive research, I've concluded that the answer is a resounding "yes." My hope is that after you finish this book, you'll feel the same.

INTRODUCTION

Each chapter breaks down one of eight principles that, if followed, can help you raise confident, independent, and futureproof kids capable of adapting to future change, whatever form it takes. While these principles will help them navigate childhood and school with greater ease, arguably more importantly, they will set them up for success in adulthood.

Crucially, while the principles are inspired by the way I was raised, they aren't unique to my family. During my research I've come to learn that parenting experts and academic studies have confirmed (and expanded upon) what my grandparents and parents intuitively understood. These lessons stand the test of time—and rigorous analysis.

Considering what our kids are up against, this is no small feat.

In the Future, Work Will Be *Far* Less Predictable

Ask most parents what they want for their kids, and chances are they'll say something like, "a fulfilling and rewarding life."

Fair enough. These are obviously worthy goals, and ones I want for my own three children.

The problem is, that's where the conversation usually ends. What these parents typically don't say, or can't say, is how to achieve these goals.

The premise of this book is that a successful career is essential to achieving them. That people are far more likely to find a deep sense of purpose, build healthy relationships, and experience genuine happiness when they have the financial security that comes from a rewarding career.

In contrast, adults who spend their lives struggling to make ends meet, or wondering what they would do without the financial support of a spouse, are much more likely to experience negative life outcomes, such as high levels of stress, marital difficulties, and even drug or alcohol addiction. As the Nobel Prize–winning behavioral economist Daniel Kahneman succinctly put it, "Money does not buy you experiential happiness, but lack of money certainly buys you misery."[1]

Another related premise is that in our age of ever-increasing technological disruption, the opportunity to build a successful career is far from guaranteed—certainly less so than in the past.

The conclusion, then, is that the greatest gift parents can give their children is an upbringing that fosters the skills, experience, and confidence needed to build a rewarding career (and, by extension, life).

Now, up until the early '90s, parents had little reason to worry about the career prospects of their children. While they might guide them toward higher education or encourage them to develop a trade skill, that's often all that was strictly necessary. So long as a child received a high school education and developed a reasonably strong work ethic, they would be able to find a job that provided a basic level of financial security.

Not any more. Two recent employment trends are making our children's future career prospects increasingly uncertain. The first is something you or someone close to you has likely experienced firsthand: *career volatility*.

Just a few short decades ago, it was common for someone to spend their entire working life in a single field or industry. In some cases, they may have even spent their entire career at the same company. But, things couldn't be more different today. As of 2023, the average American worker between the ages of 61 and 68 had changed jobs roughly *twelve* times over the course of their career, according to the U.S. Bureau of Labor Statistics.[2]

INTRODUCTION

Even employees who stay in a single role today can find themselves having to navigate considerable change. A willingness to upgrade one's skills through retraining programs or professional development courses is increasingly a requirement if you want to get ahead (or even stay in place). The point is, fewer and fewer jobs in the modern economy set workers up for a lifetime of career security.

This process has been going on for a while. But the other, *much bigger* trend is just getting started. Many parents remain unaware of it and, as a result, are wholly unprepared for its impact on their children's lives.

This second trend is *career disruption*. It's being driven by rapid advancements in automation and artificial intelligence (AI) and is already causing a growing number of workers to be pushed out of once-stable, well-paying careers.

This accelerating shift is now affecting blue-collar and white-collar jobs alike, with traditionally "safe" industries like law, finance, and even medicine being affected in surprising ways. A 2019 study in the journal *Nature Medicine*, for instance, found that automated computer systems were more effective at detecting lung cancer in CT scans compared to human radiologists.[3] Great news for patients, not so great for radiologists.

To make matters worse (for workers of the future), those impacted by automation sometimes lack the skills or confidence to retrain for a new role. So even if they're eager and willing to work, they may struggle to return to the workforce. This can have a disastrous impact on their financial stability, personal confidence, and sense of fulfillment. Needless to say, this is not something we want our kids to experience: being heavily invested in a career only to have it pulled out from under them with no clear sense of how to move forward.

New advancements in robotics, AI, and other disruptive technologies are being uncovered every day. These changes will continue to transform industries, often in unpredictable ways. This is just as true for tasks or jobs that have historically proven difficult to automate.

Automotive repair is a good case study. Gas-powered engines are highly complicated machines, and fixing them requires a large degree of hand dexterity and the ability to problem solve for a wide range of subtle issues. Yet, battery-powered vehicles are much simpler to diagnose and repair. As a result, the recent shift toward electric vehicles has dramatically simplified automotive maintenance for millions of people. While this particular change may have been an unintentional byproduct of environmental and technological innovation, it's an example of how the need for human workers can be sidestepped in unexpected ways.

All of this is to say that many people will continue to have their careers disrupted by technology. This won't happen to everyone, and it won't happen overnight. But it's a trend that is enormously important for us to recognize as parents, because it's going to dramatically affect the lives of our children.

The Good News

As worrying as career disruption has been and will continue to be, paradoxically, it's also paving the way toward a brighter future for our children. That's because automation primarily comes for roles that involve a tremendous amount of unfulfilling, repetitive, or mindless work. There are exceptions, of course, but most of the tasks being taken over by machines and AI algorithms are those that are unattractive to the next generation of workers.

This matters more than ever today, especially among younger workers. It used to be that financial success and social status were the strongest incentives driving career selection. People were ready and willing to sacrifice their time, health, and freedom in exchange for higher pay and a chance to move up in their organization and earn prestige. Today, however, survey after survey indicates that many younger workers place a much greater emphasis on finding purpose, connection, and meaning in their work.[4] Financial success still matters—they still have to pay their rent and want a comfortable life—but only up to a certain level.

This new outlook is well suited to a world in which automation takes on a growing share of repetitive, process-driven tasks. In the future, we'll see more of people's time and energy freed up to focus on learning new skills, connecting with people, and solving challenging problems.

Now, while this type of work can be far more rewarding, *it's not easy*. It requires people who are curious, self-motivated, eager to learn, and willing to take on difficult challenges. As a result, there will be a growing demand for people I like to describe as "curious problem solvers": those who are eager to learn new things and, in fact, take pride in their ability to adapt to new challenges.

What separates human beings from computers is our ability to solve complex, loosely defined problems. When we face a difficult challenge for the first time, we can draw on our diverse life experience, identify relevant patterns, and attempt possible solutions until we find one that works. Computers cannot yet do this. While some technologists predict a future in which AI eventually unlocks this ability, what is clear today is that this kind of problem solving is our greatest opportunity to contribute and be fulfilled, both in the workplace and our personal lives.

What to Expect from This Book

At this point, hopefully I've convinced you that (1) career success greatly improves one's odds of living a fulfilling and rewarding life,

(2) advances in AI and automation will massively upend the job market as we know it, and (3) nurturing our children's problem-solving abilities is crucial for preparing them to thrive in an increasingly unpredictable world.

If you agree—and I think most of you will—the critical question becomes: How do we make that happen? That's where the eight principles in this book come in. They provide a detailed playbook for raising kids to become adults who remain eager to learn new things and who embrace new challenges.

While the eight principles are distinct, they also overlap in powerful ways. Running through each principle is the belief that having consistent, meaningful conversations with our children is incredibly, life-changingly important. This idea supports every suggestion and recommended action.

There are countless books, articles, and podcasts that offer advice on raising kids. The overwhelming majority, however, focus on *what* to do and sometimes *why* to do it. What is often missing is a clear sense of *how*, *when*, and *where* to apply the insights in everyday life. Without these critical details, valuable advice often fails to create a lasting impact.

This book, on the other hand, is geared toward creating meaningful and lasting change. Rather than leaving you with a collection of helpful but abstract insights, the content is built around a simple dinner time habit that you can use to apply the principles on a daily basis, as we'll explore in the very first chapter.

The advice is ideal for parents whose children are old enough to participate in self-selected hobbies. This typically begins around the age of four and continues through adulthood. As long as your kids are capable of selecting and participating in various pursuits—such as sports, dance, computer programming, martial arts, or playing a musical instrument—the principles in this book will be relevant and actionable for you.

INTRODUCTION

Full disclosure: The core insights we will cover are not my own. While my wife and I are following the principles as we raise our three children, full credit goes to my parents, grandparents, and the many experts and scholars referenced throughout this book. I've compiled this resource out of a deep desire to better understand their valuable wisdom and to make it accessible to a wider audience.

Ready to begin? Let's get started.

PRINCIPLE 1

Support Kids' Growth with a Daily Routine

Effective parenting begins with nurturing meaningful relationships with our children.

Our ability to support their development is deeply connected to the level of awareness we have of their interests, challenges, and opportunities. It's not enough to simply love or care deeply about our kids; we must *connect* with them on a regular basis so we can understand what they're going through and how we can support their growth and development.

A child will have many teachers, coaches, or mentors over the course of their lives. Yet, as parents, we serve a unique and vital role. Not only do we tend to care more deeply about them, but we also have a more complete view of their life journey. Thus, while other adults may be involved in guiding their schoolwork, hobbies, or other specific areas of their lives, we are uniquely positioned to support their *overall* development. In a sense, we serve as the head coaches of their lives, while other adults play specialized, supporting roles.

Now, if this all sounds like common sense—that's because it is. I think most parents would agree that building a strong connection with their kids is essential—especially those who pick up a book about raising confident kids. But recognizing the importance of connection is one thing; turning that understanding into action is another challenge entirely.

Life can get busy, and we can easily lose sight of this critical responsibility. If we aren't proactive about developing a relationship with our kids, our role can become limited to that of supervisor, taskmaster, or—worse—disciplinarian. Instead of connecting with them on a personal level, we can find ourselves doing little more than establishing boundaries, providing feedback, and managing the household. Yes, these things are important, but they should not define the relationship we have with our children.

Consistency Is Key

As part of a family of six with four growing boys, my parents had a lot to manage. Yet, no matter how busy things were on any given day, *family dinner* was a stable and consistent part of our routine. It was where some of our most valuable conversations took place. Every night, we would share things that were going well, vent about challenges or setbacks, and discuss ways to make progress toward our goals in life. And we did so whether we wanted to or not, whether we were feeling happy or frustrated, content or annoyed.

Dinner wasn't the only time we would have meaningful talks. There were great conversations during long road trips, one-on-one chats while engaging in various hobbies, and other opportunities to connect with our parents. However, dinner conversations were unique because, with rare exceptions, they were a *consistent* part of our daily lives.

Of course, the idea that dinner is a great time for family conversations is hardly new. For as long as people have been gathering around a table (or even a humble cooking fire), dinner has served as a time for families to come together and connect. The tradition cuts across many diverse cultures throughout human history. However, the popularity of this practice does seem to be declining in recent years. In our busy, hectic, overscheduled modern world, fewer families get together for dinner every day, and those who do are often too distracted to engage in meaningful conversations.

Between longer work hours, expanding social obligations, and addictive technologies like social media, it can be hard to be fully present for casual yet meaningful conversations with our kids. However, I firmly believe that now, more than ever, we need to prioritize the practice of setting aside and protecting time for this kind of valuable routine.

It may be impractical for some families to maintain a routine around family dinner. Perhaps a parent works an evening shift or a child has extracurricular activities that create a scheduling conflict. That's okay. The key is to *find a consistent routine that works for you.*

For some, it may be best to get everyone together for family breakfast. For those who drive their kids to school, the daily commute may be an attractive option, albeit one that only occurs five days a week. Finally, for parents with young children who are prone to distraction at the dinner table, it may be easiest to chat with each child individually as part of an extended bedtime routine. What matters most is that we set aside time to engage in meaningful conversations with our kids as an *automatic* part of our regular schedule.

We don't have to be perfect parents on any given day, but we do have to show up consistently. Doing so helps us turn the fuzzy goal of "being a great parent" into a simple commitment to be present and engaged each day.

The importance of making this routine can't be overstated. As James Clear explains in *Atomic Habits*, "You do not rise to the level of your goals. You fall to the level of your systems."[5] Given this reality, we must build a reliable system that allows us to consistently nurture strong relationships with our kids.

The ultimate goal is to have our children associate dinner time, or whatever other daily block of time we designate, with conversation. Everyone in the family will come to anticipate that it's a time to share challenges, lessons, or other details about their lives with the family.

Over the coming chapters, we'll explore various ways to make the most of these conversations. But for now, our focus is on simply establishing a daily routine to ensure we're able to have them.

Be Casual and Convenient

There are several important considerations to make when choosing the best time and place for your routine. To illustrate them, we'll first explore why dinner time is such an excellent opportunity to connect. That way, even if dinner is not a fit for your schedule, you'll know what to look for in an alternative.

First and foremost, dinner is a casual and comfortable group environment.

There are minimal expectations or pressures when chatting during a family meal. Kids can participate as much or as little as they like, depending on the theme or the flow of the conversation. In contrast, going out of your way to schedule a formal "family meeting" is more likely to result in an awkward or uncomfortable discussion, with children feeling like they've been put on the spot.

Second, for most people, eating dinner together is already a well-established routine.

As a general rule, it's much easier to build upon an existing habit than to start a brand-new one. Furthermore, dinner typically occurs at the same time and place each day, making it an exceptionally strong routine. So rather than starting a new ritual from scratch, we can instead get more out of this reserved time by being intentional about how we use it.

Finally, dinner is built on a universal need that is constant.

Unlike other habits or routines that may come and go, dinner isn't going anywhere. Everyone needs to eat. Therefore, dinner is a rock-solid foundation on which to build a valuable, long-lasting habit of engaging in meaningful conversations with our kids.

Of course, dinner isn't the only opportunity that meets this criteria. For some, breakfast or lunch may be more attractive. And for others, there may be another time that is a better fit. Once again, the key is to *find a time that works for you*, so that family conversations become an automatic part of your daily routine.

Note: For consistency and brevity, the following chapters will use "dinner time" to refer to the activity anchoring your daily routine, but the advice offered can easily be adapted to any routine you establish as an alternative.

Getting Everyone on Board

Parents with young children have it relatively easy. They can quickly establish a new dinner routine with little fuss or pushback. Likewise, families with a strong tradition of eating dinner together have little to do but alter the way they make use of this time. However, establishing a new routine can be more challenging for parents of older kids who are less accustomed to getting together for family meals.

This is especially true when other dinnertime behaviors have become established, such as watching television, messaging with friends, or taking a plate of food to eat elsewhere. It can be a real challenge to get everyone on board with the idea of sitting together around the dinner table without distractions. In such cases, you have two options: (1) You can either select another time that may be a more natural fit or (2) you can work to create a new dinner routine centered around bringing the family together. If you choose the latter option, here are three important steps you can take to improve your odds of success.

Step 1 – Get all participating adults on the same page.

You may have a spouse, live-in grandparents, or other relatives that eat dinner with you and your children. It's critical that they understand the many benefits of engaging your kids in meaningful conversations, and that they are willing to participate alongside you. I encourage you to work with them to identify a consistent time for family dinner. It's much easier to start a new dinner routine with their full, enthusiastic support.

If they refuse, or agree in principle but fail to follow through, consider establishing an alternative routine that reliably works for you and your children.

Step 2 – Invite your kids to participate in a trial period.

Every family situation is unique. Accordingly, there is no one-size-fits-all strategy for proposing a new dinner routine. However, as a general rule, it's better to start the process by letting your kids know about your sincere desire to connect with them rather than beginning with demands or coercion. By communicating your wish to learn more about their lives and interests, you make it easier to later pivot to another routine that may be a better fit.

With this in mind, I recommend you propose a three-week trial period, after which everyone can reassess how things are going. Be sure to acknowledge that this is a *big* request, especially if your kids are used to other routines during dinnertime, such as watching television. Of course, they may still not be up for it, in which case you'll need to find an alternative routine that works better for them.

Step 3 – Create an experience that is positive and rewarding.

When it comes to establishing a lasting routine, the most important thing you can do is create a positive experience for everyone involved. We'll cover a variety of tips on how to do this over the coming chapters, but you can get started by centering the conversation around your children and their interests. This typically involves asking open-ended questions, listening thoughtfully to their responses, and following up with additional questions to learn more.

While doing this, avoid the temptation to make judgments or steer the overall direction of the conversation. Instead, simply focus on what they're most excited to talk about, and then use questions to dig deeper into those subjects. Obviously, this is easier to do if you're naturally curious about their lives and their perspectives. If this isn't yet the case, one recommendation is to treat the conversation as a challenging game. Think of the details of their lives as a mystery that you are tasked with uncovering through casual questions.

Steady Consistency Beats Irregular Moments of Greatness

Hollywood movies and television dramas would have us believe that being a great parent comes down to a few critical, make-or-break moments.

Consider how my father supported my desire to pursue business at a young age. If portrayed as a Hollywood movie, the focus would likely be on the moment I was offered the choice to drop out of high school. Yet, such a narrative would fail to convey everything that led to that moment, including the years of guidance and support that made such a choice possible.

While it's tempting to romanticize turning-point moments, it's the small, consistent daily actions that have a far greater impact over the course of our children's lives. If I'm starting to sound like a broken record, it's for a good reason. When it comes to nurturing a child's development, nothing—not even individual moments of brilliant connection—beats consistent follow-through.

A powerful benefit of taking this approach is that we don't have to stress about making the most of any particular conversation. There is no pressure to "get it right" or be perfect on any given day. The value comes from showing up and being a part of the child's journey over many years.

It's exactly this kind of low-friction, almost-invisible support that makes it possible to guide a child's growth without stealing their sense of autonomy or control. We can gently encourage their development through questions and prompts while giving them space to make choices and find solutions on their own. We'll explore this approach in much greater depth in the coming chapters, but raising a child who becomes a successful adult is, to use an old but apt cliché, a marathon, not a sprint. And how do you train to win a marathon? By showing up day in and day out, even on days when you might not feel like it.

Just to be clear, as I alluded to earlier: This daily routine is *not* the only opportunity to provide support as a parent. Making the most of this blocked-out time is no substitute for being present and active in other critical moments of our children's lives. Dinner serves as the daily anchor for developing and maintaining a close relationship in other areas of life. Think of it like *base camp* or *home base*, a stable routine where our kids can connect with us no matter how busy life can sometimes get.

Taking Action on Principle 1

Support kids' growth with a daily routine. A consistent, daily routine of talking with our children is the foundation for building deeper relationships, learning about their interests, and discovering opportunities to provide support. Here are five tips to help you get started:

1. **Discuss this principle with other adults in your home.** Make sure everyone understands the value of engaging children in meaningful conversations and confirm they are willing to participate in them. If they aren't, decide how you're going to proceed.
2. **Choose a time and place for your daily routine.** Does your family already get together for family dinner? If not, do you have the option of making it the foundation of a new daily habit? Other options may include connecting during breakfast, while driving kids to school, or during an extended bedtime routine.
3. **Identify a reliable cue for starting your routine.** What occurs just prior to family dinner? Does someone call "dinner time" to bring your family together? If not, is there another trigger word, phrase, or action that can remind everyone it's time to get ready and make the most of this time together?
4. **Set clear expectations and boundaries.** Look for ways to protect this time from distractions, such as watching

television, messaging with friends, or taking phone calls. Establish a clear precedent that this time is set aside for family conversations.
5. **Make it a positive and rewarding experience.** Ask your children open-ended questions, listen thoughtfully to their responses, and follow up to learn more. By focusing the conversation on their interests, you're more likely to engage them.

Speaking of their interests, let's move on to principle 2.

PRINCIPLE 2

Nurture Kids' Curiosity Through Self-Selected Hobbies

So much of what children learn is directed by others.

Schoolwork is taught by teachers. Extracurricular activities are guided by coaches or instructors. And, in many cases, a child's personal hobbies are selected and guided by parents who want to either relive their own passions or take a more active role in raising their kids.

The result is that children are spending much of their formative years being told what to do and how to do it. And to make matters worse, those guiding them often assess their potential for success based on their willingness to listen carefully, follow instructions, and meet expectations.

This might seem harmless—and in some ways, it is. However, when you consider the bigger picture, a significant issue emerges: In the modern, ever-changing economy, success increasingly hinges on the ability to think for oneself.

Today, the most successful people are *not* those who blindly follow the instructions of others. Instead, they're the ones who take initiative, ask the questions nobody else is asking, and adapt immediately when things don't go according to plan. This is not only true of entrepreneurs and other professions where risk-taking is celebrated, but for workers throughout the entire economy. As automation and AI continue to take on a growing share of repetitive, process-driven work, the ability to be *self-directed* is becoming more and more essential.

Structured Learning Is Useful, But It's Not Enough

In the past decade or two, there has been a shift in the way parents approach their children's education. Many are becoming increasingly preoccupied with various forms of *structured learning*, seeing it as the ideal way to help their children unlock new abilities and get ahead in life. As a result, their kids' lives tend to be scheduled around schoolwork and extracurricular activities that follow a highly structured approach. (And by "scheduled," I mean overscheduled. The typical American child spends about five hours a week participating in formal extracurriculars—on top of homework.[6])

One of the primary drivers behind this trend is the fear of having a child fall behind. Given, as we've discussed, how much more fast-paced and competitive society feels today, parents are understandably worried that a few developmental missteps might prevent their children from being accepted into academic clubs, athletic programs, or other valuable, college application–boosting opportunities. And this fear is stoked by the social pressure that comes from seeing other children participate in so many structured activities.

Of course, there are some very real advantages to structured learning. As an approach, it offers a clear, well-organized, and proven path for progressing through educational milestones, while also making it easier to track a child's progress. Schools make excellent use of this approach to help children develop foundational skills, including reading, writing, math, and basic science. Extracurricular programs tend to follow a similar approach for developing skills related to sports, music, or art.

However, structured learning also has significant shortcomings.

Let's review four of the biggest ones, and then in the following section, we'll explore a complementary approach that helps to better prepare our children for the unique opportunities of the future.

1. **Structured learning places too much emphasis on speed and measurement.**

Teachers are under tremendous pressure to ensure their students hit key milestones and achieve good grades. This pressure can come from several sources, including administrators who want to attract more students, parents who would be upset if they perceive their children are falling behind, and government policies that tie financial support to a school's academic performance.

The problem is that when teachers have a strong incentive to improve key metrics—such as a student's grades—the metrics often become more important than the outcomes they are intended to measure. This issue is so common in the business world that it inspired a famous maxim by British economist Charles Goodhart known as Goodhart's Law: "When a measure becomes a target, it ceases to be a good measure." That's because when something like student education is measured by grade averages, the incentive is to improve *grades*—even in ways that might actually harm educational outcomes. For example, schools may gradually make it easier to achieve passing grades by lowering their educational standards. And when it comes to standardized testing, which is supposed to level the playing field for measuring academic success, the incentive is to prepare students to be better at passing tests rather than pursuing a more holistic approach to education.

To be fair to teachers, many do their best to push back against these pressures. But, more often than not, even the best teachers are fighting an uphill battle, especially in places where classroom sizes are growing and education is underfunded.

2. Structured learning often fails to nurture deep, lasting knowledge or skill.

One of the core benefits of structured learning is that it tends to cover large amounts of information in an efficient and standardized way. The trade-off, however, is a lack of depth, and along with it, a lack of student understanding or mastery. That's because in an effort to make things easier for students, knowledge and skills are often isolated or abstracted away from real-world situations. So, students often end up studying facts, learning about concepts, and even developing skills—all without gaining the practical experience that would make them truly useful.

We'll talk more about this shortly, but the key takeaway here is that structured learning tends to prioritize *speed* and *ease* of learning over providing students with deep, *transferable knowledge* (that is, knowledge a student can successfully apply, on their own, to a new situation or context). The unfortunate reality is that much of what is covered in structured learning is shallow and quickly forgotten. In many ways, this kind of learning is the fast food of education, where convenience and efficiency is prioritized over lasting value.

3. Overuse of structured learning can prime a child for a life of dependence.

Kids who spend the majority of their formative years in learning environments that are overly structured can have their sense of personal autonomy diminished over time. They can grow increasingly reliant on parents, teachers, coaches, and other authority figures when it comes to making choices and knowing what to focus on next. As a result, they may struggle to take personal responsibility later in life.

For example, this kind of upbringing can cause them to delay moving out of their parents' home. It can make it more likely that they will get stuck in a dead-end career, uncertain of what they should do differently. It can make them more likely to stay with a spouse who is physically or emotionally abusive. And, if given the opportunity, it can make them more susceptible to joining a cult or an extremist group, having grown comfortable with (or at least able to tolerate) handing control of so much of their life to others.

Now, to be clear, this dependence isn't a direct result of participating in structured learning. Rather, it's caused by an absence of *unstructured* learning—opportunities in which a child gets to exercise greater independence and develop a stronger sense of autonomy. When a child's life is overly scheduled with structured learning, there's not much room left for anything else.

4. Structured learning can slowly diminish a child's natural curiosity.

All kids are born curious with a desire to learn, explore, and make sense of the world. In fact, a child's eagerness to make sense of their surroundings begins almost immediately after birth. Some infants and toddlers are so curious they often get themselves into danger. That's because their desire to learn and explore is not yet restrained by a healthy concern of physical consequences. They simply try things until they experience pain or discomfort and, in many cases, even a little pain isn't enough to derail their curiosity.

They have an *internal* motivation to want to master new skills and discover how things work; we don't have to instill this drive into them. However, an overly structured learning environment can slowly erode these *intrinsic* motivators in favor of weaker alternatives. For example, a child may become motivated to achieve an assigned outcome primarily to meet the expectations of their parents or avoid embarrassment. As opposed to being motivated by the sense of satisfaction and pride that can come from learning new things or achieving a personal goal.

Over time, these kinds of substitute motivations can cause learning to feel more like work: something that must be done, not for its own sake, but as a way to achieve other outcomes. And this in turn can cause them to start dreading opportunities to learn, even when it comes to the many subjects they would otherwise find interesting and enjoyable.

Now, again, it's important to be clear: There are very real advantages to structured learning. It offers an effective way for kids to develop foundational skills at school and during well-run extracurricular programs. But if we want to raise truly resilient, problem-solving kids who turn into resilient, problem-solving adults, structured learning must be paired with another approach, one that is better suited to nurturing curiosity, developing perseverance, and enhancing a child's sense of confidence.

Children Need Opportunities to Pursue Self-Selected Hobbies

Personal hobbies are the ideal training ground for kids to start developing life experiences that will serve them in childhood, young adulthood, and later, their working lives. This is especially true of *self-selected hobbies*—the activities a child not only decides to participate in but also actively chooses to pursue in their free time. We as parents can support and encourage these hobbies by creating time and space for them, but it's critical that children have the freedom to choose them on their own.

Of course, self-selected hobbies sometimes benefit from structured learning. For example, a child who enjoys playing soccer might also choose to participate in a soccer development program, or a kid who loves playing the guitar may want to take lessons so they can learn to play their favorite songs. The key difference is that their interest doesn't stop there. They invest some of their free time participating in the activity with friends or practicing on their own outside of structured learning environments.

To some, the idea of self-selected hobbies may sound appealing in theory but also raise some questions or concerns. I've talked to parents who worry that if they don't choose structured activities for their children, their kids may end up bouncing from interest to interest without learning much or truly dedicating themselves. Consequently, many parents strongly believe that the best way to give a child a head start is to push them to master an instrument, a popular sport, or another respected skill—and as early as possible.

These are all reasonable concerns, and we will address them shortly. But first let's explore three powerful benefits of self-selected hobbies.

1. Hobbies help deepen knowledge introduced in structured learning.

Self-selected pursuits provide kids with an opportunity to apply skills and knowledge in the real world. A child interested in studying player statistics on the back of sports cards, for instance, will have an immediate use for basic math skills. Likewise, a child who enjoys having mystery stories read to them will benefit from developing their own reading skills.

It's critical to point out that the goal of this process isn't just creating opportunities to apply academic skills. That's important, of course. But the real benefit comes from turning isolated or abstract knowledge into useful and transferable abilities. The child who applies basic math to study an athlete's statistics isn't just using what they learned in school—they are deepening their understanding of it. And every time they apply that skill in a new context, they broaden their awareness of how it might be useful in other situations as well.

Furthermore, as a child begins to appreciate how academic learning can complement their interests, they are more likely to be engaged in the classroom. It's a virtuous cycle. As parents, we can make this connection more explicit by highlighting the ways that skills they have learned, or are learning, can help them get even more enjoyment out of their self-selected hobbies.

2. Hobbies offer opportunities to practice making choices and taking initiative (and a bit of risk).

Unfortunately, many parents seem to assume their kids will suddenly develop great decision-making skills when they move out on their own. Or, at the very least, they will have an opportunity to do so in their mid-to-late teens. But the ability to make confident, independent decisions is a skill like any other. Mastery of this skill can only come from gaining practical experience in making choices, good and bad. The earlier this process begins in a child's life, the more capable they will be at working through difficult decisions later in life—and, just as importantly, dealing productively with the fallout from poor choices.

Self-selected hobbies provide children with a low-stakes environment in which they can exercise independence. While structured learning tends to reward those who follow instructions and meet expectations, hobbies provide kids with an opportunity to take the initiative and make meaningful choices.

3. Hobbies are an ideal training ground for developing perseverance and confidence.

In my experience, perseverance comes in two distinct forms. The first is primarily driven by outside influences. Someone may be able to overcome significant adversity if the reward is meeting the expectations of a teacher, parent, boss, or some other authority figure. While this kind of perseverance is certainly useful, it's somewhat limited in that it is linked with *external* motivators; that is, forces that are outside oneself.

The second kind of perseverance is more closely linked with one's sense of personal autonomy. It's driven by *internal* motivators, such as someone's passion for what they do, a desire to master a new skill, or craving the feeling of satisfaction that comes from overcoming adversity. It's this second form of perseverance that tends to get neglected in structured learning environments. Yet it's arguably much more powerful, because it can be applied to one's own interests and goals.

Self-selected hobbies are perfect for helping children develop this second form of perseverance. That's because, by their very nature, these pursuits are driven by *internal* motivators. When a child chooses to pursue a goal related to an interest they've developed on their own, it represents an achievement they genuinely want. This, in turn, makes it that much more likely they will persevere in the face of adversity and, ultimately, develop their capacity for this form of perseverance.

How Self-Selected Hobbies Help Children Develop Confidence

Every parent wants to raise confident kids. Some attempt to do so by offering their children words of encouragement or praise. Others do their best to protect their kids from failure, steering them away from challenges that might shake their positive self-image. These approaches may be well-meaning, but research conclusively shows that they often have the opposite effect.[7] The key to building a child's confidence is in helping them discover their innate ability to overcome difficult challenges.

It's inevitable that children will face many obstacles, setbacks, and even failures. Naturally, some of these experiences have the potential to be more devastating and overwhelming than others. So it's essential that we use the relatively minor challenges that a child faces earlier in life as an opportunity for them to discover their capacity for persevering in the face of adversity. It's one thing for a child to be *told* that they are clever, capable, or adaptable. It's another thing for them to witness these traits in themself as they overcome progressively more difficult challenges.

Self-selected hobbies are the perfect way to begin this process, since they give children an opportunity to face manageable challenges. Here's a simple five-stage model that outlines how the process tends to unfold.

The Five Stages of Confidence Building

Stage 1 – Curiosity. At this first stage, kids are only vaguely interested in something new they have discovered. It might be an activity they find intriguing, a skill that seems interesting, or even a promising new hobby. They aren't yet motivated to invest much time or energy, but they're curious to learn more, perhaps by watching others or participating in a casual way.

Stage 2 – Engagement. If their initial curiosity was rewarded in some way, they may choose to engage further by participating again or even committing to learning a related skill. Whatever the case may be, this second stage involves making a choice to take things to the next level.

Stage 3 – Challenge. If their interest continues to blossom, they will eventually experience a frustrating setback, difficult challenge, or some other form of failure. This is an inevitable part of any worthy pursuit, because as someone's ambition grows it will eventually exceed their current capabilities. In other words, they will reach a point at which they lack the skill, experience, or knowledge to achieve a desired outcome.

Stage 4 – Perseverance. If they care deeply about the goal or outcome, they will do what it takes to persevere in the face of adversity. This may involve upgrading their skills, rethinking their approach, or—in some cases—simply mustering up the courage to try again (and again) with greater effort. Of course, a child may also decide to abandon the process altogether at this stage.

Stage 5 – Success. If a child chooses to persevere in the face of adversity, they will experience success. When this happens, their sense of personal confidence grows. Every time they arrive at this hard-won stage they will witness how perseverance pays off, strengthening their resolve and increasing their capacity for taking on bigger challenges, and surmounting bigger frustrations, in the future.

Critically, this is a process that children must experience for themselves. They can take inspiration from the success of others (a topic we'll explore further in principle 4), but the real value of the process comes from attempting to work through each of the five stages on their own.

Now, it may be tempting to assume that a parent's role is to prevent their children from quitting this process early or, alternatively, ensuring a child only starts things they are likely to finish. But both of these approaches discourage curiosity and exploration. Once a child realizes they will be expected to commit to everything they start, they'll be less likely to share their budding interests, especially if they're not sure they're ready to commit. Worse still, they may stop exploring new hobbies or activities altogether.

It seems counterintuitive, but one of the best ways to help a child develop perseverance is to first let them experience and quit many things. Children need to discover through trial and error the pursuits that are worthy of their perseverance. They need a chance to find the activities for which their passion and curiosity are strong enough to fuel their willingness to persevere.

Our role as parents is to provide an environment that allows our children ample time and space to explore many interests and find subtle ways to support their pursuits. In doing so, we can help them discover their strengths, gain practical life experience, and build a genuine sense of personal confidence.

Help Them Discover New Interests

My parents were always curious about the interests of their four boys. While they had their own hobbies that they would occasionally share with us, they were more focused on identifying the things we were curious about. So instead of pushing us into predetermined hobbies, they found ways to support the things we wanted to do.

In talking with my father more recently, I learned my grandfather had the same approach. He was curious about understanding his children's interests, and he never pushed his own agenda on them. Instead, he would look for ways to support their hobbies while being careful never to take the lead or disrupt their sense of autonomy.

As my father and grandfather understood, a parent cannot provide helpful guidance or support until they have a clear sense of what their child is interested in and what they may be trying to accomplish. So, as we engage in meaningful conversations with our children, as covered in principle 1, we must ask questions that help us learn more about their interests: How are they spending their free time? What hobbies or activities do they seem to enjoy talking about? And, over time, how are their passions changing or evolving?

Some parents may find that their children aren't yet showing an interest in self-selected hobbies. After all, it's quite common for younger kids to default to the interests of their parents or peers. One simple way to encourage this is by putting kids into situations and environments where they can stumble upon new activities they might otherwise never encounter. For example, my parents went out of their way to take us to sporting events, local science exhibits, the public library, theater performances, concerts, the zoo, the aquarium, and even just camping in the woods. And of course, we also encountered other extracurricular activities at school, such as sports, musical instruments, and games like chess.

That may sound like an intimidating list of options, but these experiences took place over many years. It wasn't as if my parents were constantly carting us from one activity to the next. Instead, they were intentional about changing things up over the years to slowly expose us to a wide variety of potential interests. While some of these activities certainly cost money, many were inexpensive or even free. The most important thing they had was a commitment to exploring new possibilities.

Most of the potential hobbies I encountered ended at the curiosity stage. I found many of them enjoyable, but most didn't blossom into lasting interests. Yet, it was only by test-driving so many options that I was able to find the hobbies that did eventually resonate with me. And those were the activities that gave me repeated chances to push through the Five Stages of Confidence Building we just covered.

What's clear to me today is that it's impossible to predict what a child will find most interesting or most rewarding. Furthermore, we can't anticipate the impact that serendipity will play in their life. A single chance encounter with an activity or hobby can blossom into a lifelong passion, promising career, or both.

For example, one of my younger brothers decided one day that he wanted to take up playing the drums. I recall coming home and being surprised to find the drum set. For some reason, I had assumed that loud instruments were off-limits in our house, despite my parents generally being supportive of our interests. Almost from the moment I saw the kit, I became obsessed with playing it. My brother ended up focusing on other things, but I went on to take private lessons from a number of instructors. One of those instructors ended up being Jared Falk—my eventual cofounder of Drumeo, the business that went on to become the market leader in online drum education. And that in turn served as a gateway for us to launch similar businesses for helping people learn guitar and piano.

Again, the lesson here is that we never know how a chance encounter with a random hobby might transform a child's life. All we can do is plant seeds of serendipity by providing our kids with opportunities to encounter new hobbies or interests, then observe which of those seeds blossom based on their unique strengths and preferences.

NURTURE KIDS' CURIOSITY

way that allows for unexpected answers and interesting follow-up discussions.

Here are some quick examples of open-ended questions:

- What's your favorite thing to do in your free time?
- What got you first interested in basketball?
- What do you enjoy most about playing the game?
- What's the most challenging or difficult part?
- Do you have a favorite player?
- Why are they your favorite?
- What skills are most important in basketball, and why?

Again, this approach is most effective when you are genuinely curious about your children's answers. It's not about peppering them with endless questions. Rather, the goal here is to start a meaningful discussion that gives them an opportunity to open up about their interests, so you can learn new and unexpected details about them.

Sometimes the best thing you can do after asking an open-ended question is to just let them talk. If they're passionate about a subject, they may simply run with it—or even start asking questions of their own. And if you have other children, they may chime in as well. Whatever you do, avoid the temptation to steer or rush the conversation in some predetermined direction. Instead, simply take in the details and silently consider how you can learn even more or how you might support their ambitions.

Some kids may not feel comfortable answering these kinds of questions right away. So if you have multiple children, it may be best to start with one who's likely to have a ready answer. Then, as the conversation blossoms, you can invite others to participate.

Most important of all, don't overthink this. You'll learn a lot by simply engaging in the process and figuring out the kinds of questions that work and those that don't. If all you accomplish in any given conversation is you learn a little bit more about your kids, it will have been time well spent.

Children Should Be the Heroes of Their Own Pursuits

It's critical that a child's self-selected hobbies remain *self-directed*. One of the fastest ways to derail their interest or disrupt their independence is to step in and hijack the process. This can happen even if we have the best of intentions. Imagine, for instance, a child expresses interest in playing the piano. Duly motivated, we go ahead and sign them up for lessons or upgrade their keyboard with a brand-new model, all without asking.

We have to be careful that our support never overshoots the child's own level of commitment. A simple rule captures this insight: *Never be more committed to your children's hobbies or goals than they are.* So if they are *casually* interested in a new hobby, we can match that enthusiasm by creating a few new, low-stakes opportunities for them to explore it further. And, if they ramp up their commitment, we can find new ways to steadily increase our level of support to match.

The reason this approach is so important relates to the psychology of achievement. Every child deserves the opportunity to be the hero of their own journey. When we swoop in to try to set them up for success, we can unintentionally rob them of the opportunity to succeed on their own. And, in situations where they may just be casually exploring a new interest, our excessive support can put them in an awkward position, one where they feel obligated to stick with something that they may not be genuinely interested in.

This phenomenon is just as true in the classroom. Numerous studies have found that when kids are allowed to have a say in their schoolwork and how to approach it, they get better grades and have fewer conflicts with peers. Whatever the setting, kids benefit from having agency: the belief that their own actions drive their successes or failures.[8]

So, it's much better to follow a child-led approach when it comes to supporting their hobbies. Instead of proactively offering assistance whenever they show an interest in something, we can find subtle ways to be supportive while we wait for them to make a request. And, instead of immediately delivering on larger requests, we can come up with a strategy that allows them to earn that support (in effect, a way for them to *feel more responsible* for the support they receive).

For example, a child who is passionate about building model cars may ask a parent to purchase a new model for them. Instead of just gifting it to them, a parent might instead give them a chance to earn it by completing a household task that isn't part of their normal chores. That way not only will the child learn to be selective about making large requests—since they cost more time and effort—but the child will also have an opportunity to demonstrate their commitment, bolstering their perseverance.

Taking Action on Principle 2

Nurture kids' curiosity through self-selected hobbies. This will provide them with opportunities to pursue their interests, develop perseverance, and strengthen their independence. Here are four tips to get started:

1. **Use open-ended questions to learn about a child's budding interests.** We can't provide useful support until we have a clear sense of what they are trying to accomplish. Open-ended questions create opportunities for them to surprise us with new information about their interests, hobbies, or goals.

2. **Dig beneath the surface to uncover specific details about their hobbies.** By asking follow-up questions, we can learn more about the origin of their interest, their related aspirations, and what they like most about an activity or pursuit. This knowledge puts us in a better position to offer useful support.
3. **Help them identify ways to apply academic skills to their interests.** This not only allows them to deepen their understanding of what they learn in school (or other structured learning environments), but also provides them with a reason to be more engaged in the classroom.
4. **Support their hobbies without disrupting their sense of autonomy.** Avoid the temptation to swoop in and set them up for success. Instead, wait for them to ask for support and then provide opportunities for them to earn what they need, ensuring they stay invested in the outcome.

Naturally, this is an ongoing process. A child's interests and hobbies change over time—sometimes in unexpected ways. If we don't take the time to check in regularly, we may lose sight of what truly matters to them. So, while not every dinner conversation needs to revolve around their latest pursuits, it's important to return to this topic on a regular basis.

Those ever-changing hobbies and interests are the focus of our next principle. More specifically, why the more diverse they are, the better.

PRINCIPLE 3

Build Flexible Knowledge Through Diverse Experience

Many parents believe the best way to give a child a head start in life is by pushing them to begin mastering a sport, an instrument, or some other promising skill *as early as possible.*

Other parents are less worried about having their kids commit to a single skill, but still encourage their children to narrow their focus to a handful of promising hobbies early on. This tends to be driven by a belief that kids need to follow through on fewer things to achieve more meaningful progress and develop perseverance. It's also seen as a way to boost a child's confidence, by having them progress faster and further than kids who jump from activity to activity.

Some of these parents may be inspired by stories of world-class performers, such as Tiger Woods, who famously walked the golf course with his dad at the ripe age of two. There's also Wayne Gretzky, Venus and Serena Williams, and other sports greats who clearly benefited from getting an early start. Some parents may have also noticed that people who develop highly specialized skills tend to earn more money and be more successful in an increasingly competitive world. Yet, while it's certainly beneficial to develop unique skills or knowledge, starting this process too early is far more likely to put most kids at a *disadvantage* later in life.

Let's explore why.

Specializing Too Early Can Have Serious Trade-Offs

It's easy to point to examples of world-class performers who presumably succeeded because they narrowed their focus from a young age. But the truth is that making an intense early commitment like they did is a risky strategy with a low chance of success.

To start, it involves pushing a child to go all in on a pursuit without knowing in advance if (1) they'll maintain the passion needed to stick with it for years to come, and (2) their natural strengths or life circumstances will allow them to outperform potential rivals in the future.

Some might argue that it's okay even if things don't work out perfectly. After all, parents always have the option to pull back when it becomes clear their child isn't destined to be the next Wayne Gretzky or Serena Williams. But the trade-offs of such an approach can be costly.

When a child is pushed to narrow their focus from a young age, they have far fewer opportunities to explore other hobbies and interests. This in turn limits their ability to gain the diverse life experience that is essential for developing creativity, adaptability, and other problem-solving skills. Worse still, they can end up feeling stuck in an early hobby or pursuit simply because they feel so invested in it, hindering them from exploring other interests over time.

Kids Need Diverse Life Experience

As we covered in the last chapter, the ability to transfer insights from one context to another is an essential tool for solving everyday issues, big and small. It allows us to take on challenges we've never faced before by borrowing lessons from similar experiences. This is a key difference between *human intelligence* and *artificial intelligence*—and it's why we have the capacity to be more flexible than modern AI systems when it comes to dealing with unexpected challenges.

Key to helping children develop this ability is encouraging them to pursue diverse experiences. This initiates a virtuous cycle where they're able to face a greater variety of challenges, collect a wider range of life lessons, transfer some of those lessons to new contexts, and, as a result, develop a mental toolbox of *flexible knowledge* that prepares them to take on even bigger challenges in the future.

Here's an example. Picture a kid playing chess. One day, after a series of frustrating losses against a friend, they stumble upon a simple but incredibly useful insight: Rather than focusing entirely on strategies for winning more games, sometimes it's more useful to address the mistakes causing their losses. Years later, they've taken up exercise to lose some weight and get in better physical shape. After some initial progress, they start to plateau. At that point it occurs to them to apply the same basic insight they learned while playing chess. Rather than pursuing an even more aggressive exercise program to burn more calories, they decide to focus instead on addressing the bad habits that led to weight gain in the first place, such as eating fast food or spending too much time sitting in front of the television.

This example illustrates the principle of *inversion*: the idea that instead of just thinking about what causes success, it can be just as helpful to think about what causes failure. It's also a good example of a flexible insight that can be discovered in one context and transferred to another. Critically, these kinds of lessons tend to be easier to transfer after being hard-won during a meaningful pursuit. And, every time someone finds a way to apply such an insight to a new context, the core lesson becomes highlighted in their mind, making it more likely they will find further uses for it.

There are countless mental models like inversion that can be applied, successfully, to wildly varying life scenarios. But while it may be tempting to have a child just memorize a list of popular mental models, this will be largely ineffective for the same reason that academic learning often fails to stick. That's because *abstract insights are only useful to the degree that they are linked to relevant life experience.* There is little point in memorizing a list of mental models without also developing an intuitive sense of how and where they can be applied. And the best way to foster this intuition is by accumulating diverse life experience.

Consider how young children pick up new words and expand their vocabulary. Rather than studying the dictionary or memorizing lists of words, they learn through everyday interactions. When they encounter an unfamiliar word, they might ask for its meaning or use context clues to make sense of it. From there, they experiment by mimicking the way others use it to refine their understanding. Their attempts aren't always perfect—and often result in amusing phrases—but this trial-and-error process helps them grow.

Critically, as children learn to use new words in various contexts, their understanding deepens significantly. Take the word "dog," for example. For most adults, it serves as a mental representation for a complex mammal with well-defined traits and behaviors. Yet the first time a child hears the word, they might think of it as merely a nickname for their specific pet. It's only when they encounter other animals called "dogs" and notice the traits they share that they begin to grasp the word's full descriptive power.

The same is true of virtually everything we learn. Every word, concept, or insight we hold in our heads sits on a spectrum from shallow or isolated understanding to deep or abstract understanding. Initially an insight may be viewed as only being useful in a very narrow context, such as chess. But as opportunities to transfer it to new contexts arise, it can slowly morph into *flexible knowledge*, transforming from a highly specialized tool to one that can be applied to an endless number of life's challenges. As David Epstein, the author of *Range*, puts it, "Breadth of training predicts breadth of transfer."[9]

The lifelong journey of acquiring and developing flexible knowledge is messy and unpredictable. There is no perfect formula for how much time a child should spend on one activity versus another to maximize their learning. What is clear, however, is that kids need ample opportunity to develop skills and knowledge across a variety of contexts. So when it comes to helping our children develop a mental toolbox for solving complex problems, our first priority should be making it easier for them to acquire diverse experiences. Specialization can come later, as we'll soon discuss, but we shouldn't rush to narrow a child's focus too early.

People Who Can Solve Tricky Problems Will Always Be in Demand

Problem-solving skills are often undervalued, largely because they aren't a primary focus in many traditional hobbies and activities. Take playing a sport or musical instrument, for example. In each, the emphasis is typically on practicing specific physical movements or memorizing established patterns and techniques. These activities fall into what psychologist Robin M. Hogarth calls "kind learning environments," situations where goals are well defined, patterns repeat in predictable ways, and feedback is quick and highly accurate.[10]

For example, when a musician attempts to perform a particular song, they either play the right notes, with the right technique, in the right sequence—or they don't. The objective is very clear, so it's easy for a qualified teacher to assess their performance and provide instant and accurate feedback. The same is true when it comes to improving one's ability to play chess and, to a lesser degree, when it comes to team sports, like basketball and hockey. In these cases, the objective of the game is clear and one's ability to play at a high level involves mastering well-understood skills and learning to respond correctly in common or predictable scenarios.

It's the opposite in what Hogarth calls "wicked learning environments." In these situations, information is often hidden, and feedback may be delayed, infrequent, nonexistent, or even inaccurate. It's often far more difficult to know if one's choices or actions will make things better or worse.

In his book *Educating Intuition*, Hogarth uses an anecdote from acclaimed New York City doctor Lewis Thomas's autobiography as a practical example. As Thomas recounts, his father, also a doctor, had a highly respected colleague who claimed he could predict when a patient was going to get typhoid well before they had any symptoms. His predictions were amazingly accurate, but not because of any special skills he possessed. As it turned out, his method of examination involved palpating his patients' tongues with his hands, leading him to transmit the disease from patient to patient. With no other form of feedback, the doctor believed he was diagnosing correctly, so he continued the harmful habit.[11]

Equally complex (but fortunately less deadly) situations are common in the modern economy. It's not unusual for someone's actions or choices to result in excellent short-term results only to later cause serious long-term issues for a business, project, or initiative. And, unlike improving one's ability to play a sport or musical instrument, there isn't always a clear path for making predictable progress. Some of the most brilliant moves in business history were judged to be mistakes at the time they were made. And conversely, some of the biggest mistakes were choices that were judged to be safe or correct in the moment.

It's understandable that, in the face of uncertainty, some people might prefer the predictability of kind learning environments. However, the most rewarding and well-paying careers often demand the ability to excel in wicked learning environments, where flexible knowledge and other problem-solving skills are key. And, as automation continues to replace repetitive, process-driven tasks, we can expect career opportunities in kind learning environments to shrink over time.

This is why it's so critical to prepare our children to thrive in wicked learning environments. And why we should encourage them to pursue the diverse life experiences they will need to hone their ability to overcome new, complex, or unexpected challenges.

Now, just to be clear, there is nothing wrong with pursuing hobbies that involve kind learning. I'm not at all suggesting you dissuade your children from playing chess or learning a musical instrument. In fact, earlier I provided an example of how flexible insights, such as inversion, can be discovered through games like chess. (Not to mention, these kinds of activities are just fun!) The point is to recognize the difference between kind and wicked learning environments, and how diverse life experiences can help kids thrive in the latter, ultimately preparing them for success in life.

The (Many) Advantages of Specializing Late

The ideal time for our kids to choose a specialized career is *after* they've explored many hobbies and interests. By delaying specialization until their mid-to-late teens, or even later in some cases, they greatly improve their odds of selecting a path with high "match quality," a term for how well (or not) someone's strengths and preferences align with their career. This approach gives them a big advantage when it comes to mastering relevant skills, staying resilient in the face of adversity, and finding more enjoyment in what they do.

Better still, by accumulating more diverse life experience prior to specializing, they are more likely to blossom into T-shaped people, a concept popularized by McKinsey analyst David Guest in a classic 1991 article about workplace skills in the *Independent*.[12] The vertical line in the capital letter "T" represents the depth of specialized skill or expertise someone develops in a single field, while the horizontal line represents their ability to work and communicate across disciplines, tapping into insights and lessons they've gained from various life experiences.

Those who are T-shaped, as opposed to I-shaped, are more flexible and better suited to solving new or unexpected challenges. They are the ones who seem to easily come up with creative breakthroughs to issues that others have struggled with for years. Their ability to do so is because of their capacity to apply flexible knowledge from other—and often unrelated—areas of life.

In an increasingly unpredictable world, leaning into a T-shaped approach is more likely to set our kids up for success. Today, it's more common than ever for people to switch from one specialized career to another, in some cases more than once over the course of their working life. By raising our children to be comfortable in many different contexts, and to have a greater understanding of their strengths and preferences, we set them up to be more adaptable to change. Whether that change is driven by unexpected career disruption or their own desire to pursue something new, they will be ready and able to handle what comes their way.

Building a Unique Talent Stack Is an Alternative to Specialization

Scott Adams, creator of the long-running *Dilbert* comic strip, has said he doesn't consider himself much of an artist or business expert. He's a self-taught writer, and he doesn't even think he's the funniest person in his town. Despite his supposed lack of talents, however, the skills he *does* possess have come together to create a rare, effective, and valuable combination that helped him stand out.

Adams credits his success to his unique "talent stack." Here's how he defines the concept in his own words: "You can combine ordinary skills until you have enough of the right kind to be extraordinary. You don't have to be the best in the world at any one thing. All you need to succeed is to be good at a number of skills that fit well together."[13] Simply put, the value of a talent stack is more than the sum of its individual parts.

This is something I've witnessed in my own life and the lives of many other successful people.

I consider myself a rather average entrepreneur. One of my unique strengths is my marketing experience, but I wouldn't consider myself in the top 10,000 marketers in the world. And, while I can play several instruments, I'm an amateur musician at best. However, these skills all came together when I cofounded three successful businesses in online music education.

The best part about this approach is that it doesn't require a master plan. Kids can start down this path by simply accumulating interesting skills and expertise, just as they might while exploring opportunities for a specialized career. Then, later in life, if it turns out that they're uninterested in committing to a single area of expertise, they can instead look to combine some of their abilities into a unique and valuable talent stack.

I never set out to learn the drums to build a related business. I was just genuinely interested in playing the instrument and even had ambitions of making music with a band. It was only later that my passion for drumming and my interest in technology and entrepreneurship came together, putting me in a position to cofound Drumeo, Guitareo, and Pianote with my business partner, Jared Falk.

Of course, had I stumbled upon a promising opportunity to specialize in online marketing before meeting Jared, my life may have gone down a very different path. That's the beauty of the talent stack–building approach: It opens up possibilities without closing doors. We never know where our children's lives may lead them, or what skills will be most useful to them in the future. But the more diverse experience they accumulate, the more options they'll ultimately have.

Taking Action on Principle 3

Build flexible knowledge through diverse experience. Doing so helps kids identify their strengths and preferences, accumulate valuable life skills, and improve their ability to solve complex problems. Here are four tips to get started:

1. **Create opportunities for kids to try new things.** It's easy for them to grow bored with the same old routine. A great way to reignite their passion for growth is to help them discover entirely new hobbies or interests.
2. **Be intentional about introducing new experiences.** It's easy to get stuck in a pattern of identifying as a *sports family*, a *camping family*, or an *artistic family*, but this can limit our children's opportunities. So it's important that we go out of our way to mix things up and introduce a greater variety of options over time.

3. **Use open-ended questions to better understand their evolving interests.** The more we know about our children's hobbies and goals, the better prepared we will be to offer appropriate support and encouragement (or, if necessary, redirection).
4. **Provide children with free time for their hobbies and let them decide how to use it.** While it's helpful to provide opportunities for them to stumble upon new interests, they should retain control over how they choose to spend their free time. Again, it's important that their hobbies are both self-selected and self-directed for all the reasons covered in the last chapter.

One of the best ways for kids to absorb these values is to see them in action, especially through the role models they encounter in their life. This important group includes their parents, their siblings, their social circle, and other inspirational figures, such as athletes, musicians, inventors, artists, or perhaps even famous businesspeople. That is the focus of the next chapter.

PRINCIPLE 4

Shape Positive Behaviors with Effective Modeling

One of the easiest parenting mistakes to make is offering kids too much unsolicited advice.

It's not hard to understand the impulse. We've learned valuable lessons over the course of our lives, many of which have the potential to make our children's lives easier or better. So it can be all too tempting to share words of advice with our kids even when they haven't asked for our help.

For example, we might encourage them to try new things, set ambitious goals, believe in themselves, persevere in the face of adversity, or not be afraid of failure. We may also go a step further and explain the benefits of following our advice or why they should take our recommendations seriously.

Unfortunately, as it turns out, unsolicited advice is largely ineffective in guiding a child's development (or an adult's for that matter).[14] Not only do kids tend to discard or ignore this kind of input, but even when our advice resonates with them, it rarely impacts their behavior in a meaningful way.

There are many reasons for this, but here are three that really stand out.

1. Unsolicited Advice Puts People on the Defensive

While very young children can be receptive to advice, this tends to change as they develop a stronger sense of autonomy. Consider what it's like to receive unsolicited advice as an adult. While we may respond politely, more often than not we silently reject the intrusion in favor of our own ideas. And if someone makes a habit of offering too much unsolicited advice, we may even grow to resent them.

So it should come as no surprise that our kids don't always appreciate it when we swoop in with opinions for how they should live their lives. While they, too, may respond politely in the moment, or even feign interest in what we have to say, they are no less likely to discard our recommendations.

2. There Can Be a Significant Knowledge or Experience Gap

While we may feel like we're offering universal or timeless advice, our children often view what we say through a variety of filters that can alter how our message is received.

For starters, they may perceive a *generational gap* that causes them to view our advice as being outdated or out of touch with the challenges they're facing. Second, they may simply fail to understand or appreciate how our advice will make their life better, as they have not had the same experiences that we've had. And third, kids tend to operate on a different time horizon, focusing more on things that affect their life *today* rather than the long-term impacts of their choices or actions over time.

3. Kids Like to Rebel Against Authority

As children begin to seek more independence, they sometimes reject the advice of others to assert their own decision-making abilities. This reaction can be so automatic at times that offering advice reliably causes them to choose a different path, often one that is the opposite of what's being recommended. This behavior isn't unique to children; adults who feel their autonomy is being threatened often respond in a similar way.

All of this is to say that, even if our advice lines up with our children's interests or intentions, they may still reject our input out of hand simply because the ideas or insights are not their own. (There are situations when our advice may be welcome, but if it is, it's most likely *been requested*.)

As frustrating as all of this may be, try to remember that we don't actually want to raise kids who blindly follow the suggestions of others. Otherwise, there is little to keep them from being manipulated by other people who may not have their best interest at heart. Instead, we want to raise our kids with a healthy sense of skepticism so they can question things, make choices for themselves, and learn from their inevitable mistakes. And the earlier this process begins—while the stakes are relatively low—the better.

So if we want to positively influence kids while helping them preserve their autonomy, we're going to have to try a different strategy.

Children Learn Best by Observing the Actions of Others

The most effective way to positively influence a child's behavior is by *modeling* the values we hope to instill in them. This is critical because kids learn best by mimicking the actions of people who are influential in their life, including parents, siblings, friends, and other potential role models. As quick as they are to discard unsolicited advice, they can be just as quick to emulate the actions, habits, and behaviors of those they aspire to be like.

Once again, there are many reasons for this, but here are four that stand out:

1. **Kids Learn Through Observation Before They Develop Language**

Long before any human was able to pass on knowledge through speech or the written word, we learned by observing and imitating others. As a result, *social learning* is more fundamental to how our brains are wired. That's not to say we can't learn through reading or conversing with others, only that learning through observation tends to come more naturally.

One key advantage to this approach is that it provides a richer level of detail than words alone. For example, it's one thing for a parent to talk about the benefits of exercise or strength training, and it's another thing entirely for a child to see how that same parent engages in various physical activities as part of a healthy lifestyle. The latter conveys a lot more context that could otherwise be missed or misinterpreted when communicated through words alone.

2. **Observing Action Is More Powerful Than Hearing Untested Advice**

Children seem to intuitively understand that, more often than not, it's both safer and smarter to see what people actually *do* rather than listening to what they *say*.

Even well-meaning people are often quick to offer advice that they themselves are unwilling or unable to follow through on. While there may be justifiable reasons for this gap, the details can be easily lost on a child. And it's generally better (and simpler) for them to emulate what they see is working for someone else than to take advice that may sound great in theory but turns out to be impractical or impossible in practice.

3. Learning Through Observation Supports Personal Autonomy

It's far more rewarding for a child to choose behaviors and values they want to emulate rather than being told how they should act. The former supports their sense of autonomy, while the latter hinders it. This may seem like a minor point, but a child who feels in control of their development (and who they are becoming) is more likely to personify the values they aspire to over time.

For example, a child who decides to follow a healthier diet after learning about their favorite athlete's eating habits is more likely to stick with it than one who's just told, "Eat your vegetables—they're good for you."

4. Children Mimic Behavior to Be Accepted

Everyone has an innate desire for connection and belonging, and this is especially true among kids. One powerful way to feel accepted as part of a group is by mimicking the values and behaviors of others who are in it. Imitation is a way to fit in and demonstrate that you belong.

Depending on the context, this can cause a child to act more like members of their family, their social circle, or some other group. In these situations, the choice to engage in a given behavior is driven by the desire to feel like part of the group, not a rigorous analysis of the advantages or disadvantages of the behavior.

There are obvious drawbacks to this. The most glaring one being that children often end up mimicking *negative* behaviors. If a parent smokes, drinks, watches too much TV, gets in constant arguments, or endlessly scrolls social media, their kids are likely to mimic these behaviors. And this is true even if the parent recommends *against* adopting some of their worst habits, which just goes to show how much more potent *social learning* (through observation) is compared to words of advice. As the old expression goes, "Actions speak louder than words."

The same is true when it comes to values or mindsets. If a parent shows no interest in learning new things, taking on new hobbies, setting ambitious goals, persevering in the face of adversity, or challenging their own beliefs, their kids are more likely to adopt a similarly passive, closed-minded approach to life.

Our Ability to Influence Is Motivating

Recognizing that our children are highly influenced by our actions and habits can become fuel for personal change. Suddenly a choice to take up running, reading, or healthier eating is no longer just a way to improve our own life. It can now be seen as a potent way to positively impact the lives of our children and perhaps the lives of our future grandchildren and beyond. This recognition can inspire us to adopt habits we otherwise wouldn't on our own.

On the flip side, this awareness can also become a source of debilitating self-criticism. It's easy to fall into the *comparison trap*, where we unfairly judge our effectiveness as parents against the best qualities we see in other parents. If we hold ourselves against this impossibly high (and false) standard, it can feel like we're *never* doing enough to model useful behaviors for our kids. Additionally, if we fail to appreciate the difficulty of changing our habits, we can set ourselves up for disappointing failure.

So before we can tap into this powerful source of motivation, it's critical that we start by recognizing that each of us is on our own journey, and we all have unique strengths and weaknesses. Furthermore, almost no parent thinks they are doing a perfect job of modeling all the values they hope to instill in their children. There are endless opportunities to improve ourselves. The best way to move forward is to accept where we are today and then look for small changes we can make to become better versions of ourselves.

As a general rule, the greatest opportunity for improvement is through eliminating our worst habits, as opposed to establishing brand-new ones. Breaking unhealthy addictions to things like smoking, drinking, social media, smartphones, or television is a deeply beneficial action, and one that tends to be more impactful than modeling positive behaviors.

While role models outside the home have the potential to inspire children with positive habits, they're less effective at modeling the *absence* of bad habits. A child is much more likely to mimic a parent's unhealthy addiction than be influenced by a favorite athlete's *lack* of the same addiction. The mere presence of an unhealthy habit in a child's home life is difficult for other role models to counteract, which is why it's so useful for us to focus first on eliminating our worst habits.

The art and science of habit change is beyond the scope of this book. However, if you're interested in learning more about breaking bad habits and building positive ones, I highly recommend you read *Tiny Habits* by BJ Fogg or *Atomic Habits* by James Clear.

Make It Easier for Kids to See the Best Version of You

There's a good chance you already have habits or routines that could positively influence your children. But if they don't notice them or understand what you're doing, these habits won't do much good. Kids need two things to imitate positive behavior: They have to see it, and they have to recognize it. After all, they can't copy what they don't observe or comprehend.

The solution is to be mindful of whether our actions are easy for them to mimic. Here's an example from my own life. I'm an avid reader, and I enjoy reading digital books while sitting on the couch as well as listening to audiobooks while doing simple chores around the house. Unfortunately, neither of these activities are effective for modeling the value of learning from nonfiction books. For one, from my children's perspective, seeing me with a tablet computer could just as easily make them think that I'm scrolling through social media or casually browsing the internet. Similarly, whenever I'm walking around the house with headphones on they have no way of knowing if I'm listening to an audiobook, a podcast, or music.

Once I realized this, I modified my behavior and altered my environment to better model my habit of reading. First, I started using a dedicated e-reader to make it easier for my kids to see when I'm reading a book. Second, I invested in physical copies of many of my favorite books. As a result, their presence throughout our home serves as a strong visual clue about the kinds of books I enjoy most. And finally, I now occasionally listen to my audiobooks through a smart speaker instead of headphones, which not only makes it easy for my kids to know what I'm listening to but may also spark a discussion on the topic being covered.

This approach—of making our best habits more observable and understandable—can be used to make almost any routine or behavior easier for children to emulate. For instance, if you normally do pushups beside your bed first thing in the morning, consider doing them near the kitchen table while your kids are having breakfast. Of course, this may not cause them to immediately follow your lead, but it helps to subtly convey your interest in exercise and healthy living.

There are endless examples. But the point is, before introducing entirely new habits, begin by taking inventory of how you already spend your time. Identify the activities or routines that have the potential to positively or negatively influence your kids. Then look for ways to make your best habits more observable while eliminating (or minimizing the visibility of) your worst ones.

Make the Link Between Positive Behaviors and Desirable Outcomes Obvious

It's easy to assume our children understand *why* we do the things we do. We may think the benefits of reading books, pursuing new hobbies, or taking on difficult challenges are obvious. We shouldn't take it for granted, however, that a child will automatically link these kinds of actions to desirable outcomes. So in addition to making some of our behaviors more visible, it's also important to help our kids connect the dots between *what* we are doing and *why* we are doing it.

Let's say that you recently had a breakthrough on a project at work, and that it was the result of an insight you picked up from a great book. Well, when it comes time to sharing highlights from your day during a family meal, instead of just saying, "Today was great! I came up with the perfect solution to a difficult problem at work," you could add some important context by explaining, "The idea was inspired by an insight I read in a book, *Essentialism* by Greg McKeown." By doing this you make the cause and effect clearer.

DINNER TIME CONVERSATIONS

Some of you might react to that example by cringing a little. Perhaps you've seen parents (including your own) turn similar conversations into awkward "teachable moments," turning a casual chat into a life lesson ("Read more books!"). The key difference here is that we simply want to add information that links a positive outcome to a certain behavior. What we do *not* want to do is make a big fuss and try to sell them on a specific habit or action. Instead, we just want to give our kids many natural opportunities to understand the benefits of our best habits. That way, as they connect the dots over the course of their childhood, they will be more likely to mimic the habits they see as useful.

Another key to effective modeling is to be open about the challenge of maintaining good habits. It can be tempting to pretend that a useful routine, like going to the gym, is *easy* or to give the impression that we always feel like doing the right thing. But this can backfire, because our kids will inevitably face some level of resistance when they attempt to follow our path. When that happens, they may end up feeling like we have some kind of unfair advantage that they lack or that they must be doing something wrong. Without understanding that habits can be difficult, they may assume they're the problem and quickly give up.

Because I'm conscious of this, on days when I don't really feel like going to the gym I might casually mention, "This is one of those days where I really don't feel like working out." Then, as I continue to get ready to head to the gym anyway, I might add something like, "But I know I'll feel so much better afterward."

The goal here is to communicate what following through on positive habits is like realistically—the good and the bad—and, critically, *why* we are willing to follow through. The same approach can be applied to struggles around eating a healthy diet, being disciplined with money, doing chores around the house, taking on a complex project, or almost anything else of value that requires effort. In each case, simply share what it feels like to struggle with taking action, and then briefly mention why you're choosing to follow through anyway. Connect the behavior to a desirable outcome, such as feeling healthier, saving money, living in a tidier home, being happier, or feeling more accomplished.

Again, we have many years to positively influence our children. So we don't need to oversell or make a big show of promoting any one value or behavior over another. Instead, we just want to model what it's *really* like to do our best to adhere to our values.

Help Kids Discover Role Models Who Share Their Interests

As I mentioned earlier, we aren't the only ones who can serve as positive role models for our children. In fact, there are times when others are far better suited for modeling certain values or behaviors. With this in mind, it's critical we look for opportunities to connect our children with other positive influences. This can take some effort on our part, but it also relieves us of the impossible burden of being an expert or role model in all areas of life.

While we don't have direct control over who our children ultimately choose as role models, we can help them discover positive influences who share their interests or life goals. For example, when my brothers and I first started playing basketball in our early teens, my father bought a box set of instructional videos featuring basketball star "Pistol" Pete Maravich. Likewise, when we started playing hockey, he took us to NHL games where we could be inspired by the amazing abilities of professional players. He didn't push us to select any specific role model, but instead provided us with opportunities to identify people who we found inspiring.

Obviously, a child may fail to show interest in a potential role model despite our best efforts; at other times, a connection may simply be delayed. But the more potential role models you expose them to, the more opportunities you create for them to connect with one.

A powerful benefit of interest-based role models is the motivation they can provide. Their initial influence tends to be an inspiring glimpse of what's possible in their area of mastery or expertise. In the case of the Pete Maravich instructional videos that my father purchased, it wasn't so much Pete's work ethic that initially stood out to me, but his creative approach to playing basketball. He served as an example of what was possible. It was only after I was inspired to pursue a similar approach that he began to influence my values and behaviors around things like work ethic and what effective practice looked like.

This links back with what we covered in principle 3, the importance of helping our children discover new hobbies. By creating opportunities for them to witness experts demonstrating their impressive knowledge or skill, we can provide the inspiration they need to make a deeper commitment. And later, when they select an ambitious goal for themselves, ongoing exposure to related experts can provide bursts of inspiration that help them overcome the various challenges they'll inevitably face.

The underlying insight here is that, rather than *pushing* our children toward specific achievements or targets, we can create opportunities for them to be naturally *pulled* toward goals or outcomes that inspire them. Not only is this more likely to lead to better results, but it also strengthens their sense of autonomy.

Identifying worthy role models begins by really listening to our children and having meaningful conversations with them, as covered in principle 1. As we learn more about their interests, we can identify potential role models by diving into videos, podcasts, or other relevant media. Whenever possible, include local experts or individuals who travel through your area so your kids can watch them perform live (and possibly even meet them).

Uncover Their Role Model's Journey

Children tend to fixate on the current abilities of their heroes. They're blown away by the impressive skills or knowledge they exhibit *today*, but generally lack insight into the journey that led to their success. This leads many kids to buy into the myth of *natural talent*: assuming their heroes were always great or that, at the very least, they were born with an unfair advantage that allowed them to learn faster than other people.

Unfortunately, such a belief can make it less likely that a child will emulate the effort, practice, and perseverance required to succeed. To help kids break free of this myth, we must build on the insight we covered earlier about the need to connect our positive behaviors with desirable outcomes.

When it comes to other role models, we need to approach the same challenge—but from the opposite perspective. This involves helping our kids reverse engineer the desirable outcomes that their heroes have already achieved. That way, they can develop an understanding of the habits, behaviors, and values that led to their success.

One good way to do this is to dig deeper into the lives of those they look up to. This might involve watching documentaries about their life, reading biographies, listening to interviews, or—when possible—directly witnessing their efforts to improve. On this last point, I recommend showing kids videos that document what it's really like to learn difficult skills.

For example, I recently stumbled upon a popular YouTube video of skateboarder Jonny Giger struggling to learn what he describes as "the hardest trick of [skateboarding legend] Rodney Mullen." Over the course of eighteen minutes, the video showcases many of Giger's 1,400+ attempts to perform the famous trick before he's eventually successful. That's a long time to watch someone fail! But there's a reason it has 1.9 million views and counting: It gives viewers—skateboarders and non-skateboarders alike—a revealing glimpse of the level of persistence it can take to master a single trick. After watching the video, you can't help but respect the hours of hard work Giger put in. So, even if you can't find a video of your child's specific role model, you may be able to find videos like this where someone else showcases what it's like to follow in their footsteps.

Obviously there's a balance to maintain here. We don't want to discourage our children by drawing attention to how challenging something can be, especially when they're just getting started. However, as their commitment level grows and they begin to identify inspiring role models, it helps to offer small glimpses into the process and effort that allowed their heroes to become successful.

As I pointed out earlier, *a child can't mimic what they can't see.* If they want to follow in their role models' footsteps, they need to witness the actions and behaviors that make success possible. Ideally, they'll get a chance to see their heroes struggle, fail, question their abilities, work even harder, and find the resolve to push through—everything they, too, will go through on their own journey. They just need to know to expect it. Or better yet, to embrace it.

Show How You Take Selective Inspiration from Others

One risk with role models is that they can serve as both a positive *and* negative influence. Their standout abilities might inspire us, but their shortcomings can sometimes be mistakenly seen as key to their success. A classic example is musicians and artists who, intentionally or not, have perpetuated the idea that creativity is linked with heavy drug use. Although this myth has fortunately faded somewhat over time, it's still strong enough that young people who look up to these figures may believe they need drugs to unlock their own creative potential.

Another example: Steve Jobs was famous for his ability to lead the development of remarkable products, like the Macintosh and iPhone. Yet it's also widely known that he was often a jerk and could be a nightmare to work with. As a result, this has led many aspiring entrepreneurs to incorrectly assume that the best way to emulate his success is to treat their employees in an equally brutal manner.

As parents, we can help our children avoid these kinds of mistakes by modeling the effective use of role models. When we talk about people who've inspired us, it's important to point to specific traits, values, or behaviors that we admire. And, rather than putting our heroes on a pedestal, we can call attention to (and reject) their flaws when appropriate. Even better, we can point to *other* role models who serve as counterexamples to the perception that such flaws are useful or necessary.

So if we've been inspired by a famous artist or musician who was known to have taken drugs, we can make a point to highlight specific traits that we admire, such as their work ethic, their willingness to push boundaries, or their showmanship, while also pointing out and rejecting their drug use. Then we can point to other creative artists or musicians who achieved similar success without drugs.

The key here is to model the idea that we're all human. Even our heroes make mistakes. We can admire them for their best traits, but we shouldn't give them a pass when it comes to their flaws. In modeling this approach for our kids, we can encourage them to emulate the best attributes from a range of inspirational figures, rather than taking both the best *and* worst of any one role model in their life.

Taking Action on Principle 4

Shape positive behaviors with effective modeling. Making it easy for children to witness useful habits and behaviors will give them a chance to learn through observation, appreciate why others do the things they do, and select the actions and routines that align with their goals or aspirations. Here are five tips to get started:

1. **Minimize or eliminate the visibility of negative influences.** This applies to things that take place both inside and outside the home. If harmful habits or behaviors are less likely to be observed, they're less likely to be mimicked.
2. **Maximize the visibility of positive influences.** Kids can't emulate what they can't see, so it's important that we go out of our way to make it easier for them to witness the positive habits of others—including ourselves.
3. **Look for opportunities to tap into the power of role models.** Instead of pushing your child to pursue predetermined goals or outcomes, help them discover talented people who can inspire them into action.
4. **Establish a link between behaviors and desirable outcomes.** One way to do this is by helping your child understand *why* you do the things you do. Another is to help them identify the habits and behaviors that allowed their heroes to accomplish great things.
5. **Serve as a role model for how to be inspired by others.** Young children tend to put their heroes on a pedestal and assume they can do no wrong. So, it's important for us to demonstrate that it's better to admire specific traits, values, or behaviors rather than people as a whole. That way,

SHAPE POSITIVE BEHAVIORS

they're less likely to fall into the trap of emulating the worst traits of their heroes.

Of course, there are times when children need direct assistance. Perhaps they are facing an obstacle or challenge that requires a more immediate solution. That's the subject of the next chapter.

PRINCIPLE 5

Nurture Problem Solving with Open-Ended Questions

It can be difficult to know what to do when a child comes to us with a challenge or problem.

On one hand, we don't want to discourage them from letting us know about the various difficulties in their life. On the other, we don't want them to grow dependent on our assistance, turning to us for help with every little issue. Otherwise, they may never learn to properly deal with things on their own.

While many parents agree with this in theory, in reality they often take steps that unintentionally limit their child's self-sufficiency. They remove obstacles, eliminate risks, and step in to help whenever a child faces a difficult challenge. For some, this is done out of a sincere yet misguided desire to help their kids learn faster, make fewer mistakes, or reach various milestones ahead of schedule. For others, this is driven by an eagerness to *look* or *feel* more effective as parents. Regardless of the motivation, this approach has a fundamental flaw: mistaking the *appearance* of development for the real thing.

DINNER TIME CONVERSATIONS

It's an easy trap to fall into, and one that can start out innocently enough. Perhaps a toddler is struggling to fit a rectangularly shaped block through a square hole. *Surely, we think, we should show them the correct approach by positioning the rectangle so the square end fits into the square hole.* So we step in to "help." After all, we don't want them to fall behind. If anything, we want them to get a head start when it comes to the mastery of shapes.

Showing them the solution, however, only addresses part of the learning opportunity. Worse, it's the *easy* part: memorizing a known solution. The missing part, the part that *really* matters, is developing the ability to work through loosely defined problems on their own. Depending on the situation, this might involve them trying several methods, failing to make progress, generating new ideas, and then eventually solving the problem. All of this is lost when we shortcut the learning process by guiding them straight to the solution.

Fortunately, no single interaction is going to make or break a child's development. However, if we continue to prioritize quick results over genuine learning we risk all kinds of unintended consequences. Kids can end up failing to develop perseverance, self-confidence, and independence, and perhaps worst of all, their natural curiosity may diminish over time. After all, why would they try to discover solutions to difficult challenges when a parent always seems ready to swoop in and do it for them?

Simply getting a child to a learning milestone is *not* as important as how they get there. Having the ability to pass a test or complete a procedure is not the same as being able to independently solve difficult problems. If we raise our kids to mindlessly memorize and follow directions, we set them up for failure in a world in which AI is becoming exponentially better at following procedures than any human.

Of course, discouraging our kids from asking for help isn't the answer, either. One way to strike a balance between the two extremes is to use questions to guide them through the process of discovering a solution on their own. The beauty of this is that it offers a way to be helpful while also modeling an approach to problem solving that kids can eventually apply without our assistance.

Questions Support Learning While Promoting Autonomy

A powerful benefit of questions is they allow us to influence the way our children think and act without stealing their sense of autonomy. Questions can challenge assumptions, shift perspectives, and expand options, while leaving room for kids to reach their own conclusions. And by relying primarily on open-ended questions, we can maximize their level of participation while avoiding many of the hazards associated with offering unsolicited advice.

The one downside of this approach is that it can be somewhat time consuming, at least in the beginning. That's because instead of pointing our children to quick and easy solutions (in the form of direct advice), we must help them think through the problem or challenge on their own. However, the process becomes much faster as children learn to home in on the critical, solution-revealing details of most problems.

The goal isn't to just help them get past a single issue. Rather, it's to give them the mental tools to deal with *any* tricky challenge. Every time we model the use of effective questions, we teach them valuable life skills, including how to identify the core of an issue, break things down into manageable chunks, and come up with a list of potential solutions.

Great Questions Are More Valuable Than Existing Answers

Education used to place a strong emphasis on memorizing known *answers*. To be successful, students needed to be able to recall answers to a wide range of questions like: *What is the capital city of Australia? What are the two stages of photosynthesis? What genus does a cat belong to?*

Today, these kinds of answers are less useful. Anyone with a smartphone is a few simple taps away from the collective knowledge of humanity. And between modern search engines and AI chatbots, it's easier than ever to discover known answers to a truly endless number of inquiries. Even the most obscure or complex subject is more approachable than ever before. As a result, the value of memorizing *answers* is in sharp decline.

Meanwhile, the ability to ask the *right questions* has become increasingly valuable. That's because one of the primary constraints on success today—at a personal, business, and even societal level—is the inability to ask truly useful questions. The ones that help us identify things worth doing *and* figure out the best ways to do them.

Unfortunately, there is a tremendous amount of waste in the world today—wasted time, wasted energy, and physical waste. Far too many people are working diligently toward goals or outcomes that were poorly thought out or are otherwise unnecessary. In some cases, people are spending countless hours trying to solve problems that have already been solved by others.

An ability to ask probing questions is a skill that helps us make better use of existing human knowledge. It helps us bring simplicity and order to things that otherwise seem to be complex and chaotic. And it helps us identify the things that really matter to us, so we can find greater purpose and fulfillment in our lives. In a world in which our children have access to a truly incredible abundance of knowledge, developing the ability to ask great questions will empower them to access the wisdom and insight of others.

The good news is that many educational systems have begun to recognize this, and their teaching practices now place a greater emphasis on the value of probing questions. There is more, however, that we can do as parents to help our children master this important skill. The first task is to sharpen our own questioning abilities so that we can serve as a useful role model for our children.

How to Use Effective Questions to Solve Difficult Problems

While every challenge is unique, there are tried-and-true methods for working through even the most complex issues. Here's a simple five-step framework we can use during casual conversations to guide our children toward a solution.

1. Seek to Understand Their Mindset and Process

Before we step in to help a child, we need to understand *why they're feeling stuck* and *what they've already tried*. We shouldn't be their first stop for every problem, so it's key to confirm they've made a genuine effort to resolve it themselves. That way, not only can we see that the issue truly matters to them but also help them identify flaws in their approach.

The next time a child presents a problem or question, consider asking, "What have you tried so far?" or "What solutions have you already considered?" You can then follow up to learn more by asking, "Why do you think that approach didn't work?" or "What do you think went wrong when you tried that?"

If it turns out they haven't yet made a real effort, you can say, "It sounds like you're just getting started on this." And then you can follow up by asking, "What do you plan to try first?" or "How do you plan to tackle that?" You may be pleasantly surprised at how often they find a solution without any help.

2. Confirm They've Identified the Real Issue

The initial question or problem may not actually be the *real* issue. It may be a symptom of some other issue, or it may just scratch at the surface of a much larger problem. Whatever the situation, it's essential that we use questions to clarify the problem and get a sense of what it will take to resolve it.

Here are some useful prompts that you can use to dig deeper:

- *How do you want this to turn out?*
- *What about that is most important to you?*
- *Tell me more about that.*
- *Are there other ways to achieve that outcome?*
- *What other options have you considered?*

While every situation is unique, more often than not this step will clarify *what they want* and *why they want it*. Knowing what they want is essential to continue to make progress. Knowing why they want it helps clarify the stakes while opening the door to alternative solutions that might be as good or better in meeting their underlying need.

3. Identify Obstacles and Areas of Uncertainty

With simple challenges that only have one primary obstacle, you may be able to skip this step and jump right into brainstorming potential solutions (step 4). Often, however, there are multiple issues preventing progress. Some may be well understood, while others may

NURTURE PROBLEM SOLVING

be caused by uncertainty or a lack of information. In such situations, it's critical that we break things down into distinct chunks.

Here are some questions that can help:

- *Can you identify smaller parts of the problem?*
- *What is one thing that is preventing you from making progress? What else?*
- *Tell me more about that. Is there anything else that comes to mind?*
- *Is there anything we've missed or might be forgetting?*
- *If you had a solution for each of the parts you've identified, would the problem be fixed?*

If a challenge is especially complex, it's useful to have the child map out each of their responses on a single piece of paper. They can start by defining the problem itself at the top of the page. Then, as individual issues are identified, they can list them down the left side of the page. (Later, when it's time to brainstorm potential solutions, they can add them to the right of each issue. That way the child ends up with a clear strategy of how to work through every aspect of the problem.)

If the list of obstacles seems to be growing out of control, this is often a signal that the problem is either poorly defined or, more likely, too large in scope. In other words, it may be too big to be tackled all at once. In such situations, it's essential to help the child zoom in on a smaller initial target—one that will help them make progress toward their larger goal while avoiding the overwhelm that can result from taking on too much at the same time.

4. Guide Them Through Brainstorming Potential Solutions

As you go over each obstacle, ask them to come up with a list of potential solutions. Or, alternatively, ask them to come up with steps they can take to uncover potential solutions. The goal is to have a clear plan for addressing each of the issues listed in the previous step. That way, rather than feeling stuck, they can build a bit of confidence, knowing they have a game plan for working through things systematically.

Here are some examples of the kinds of questions you can ask during this step:

- *What ideas do you have for tackling the first issue on the list? If that doesn't work, what else might you try?*
- *Can you think of a challenge you've faced that is similar to this? If yes, what did you learn from that experience that might be relevant here?*
- *Can you think of anyone you know who has experience with this? What questions could you ask them to get useful advice?*
- *Where might you find a step-by-step video or article on how to tackle this?*
- *What do you think about asking an AI chatbot for advice on this? What questions would you ask? If that didn't work, what else would you try?*

Again, if they are working through this process using a sheet of paper, each idea should be listed next to the obstacle it's intended to address. Some of the items will be direct solutions while others, as I hinted at earlier, will be actions they can take to start finding potential solutions. These might include asking a friend, watching a step-by-step video, or reading a how-to guide.

One thing to note: As children get better about identifying useful resources, some of the questions that point them toward potential resources can be distilled down into a single question (e.g., "Where might you find a proven solution for overcoming this issue?"). In rare cases, you may be the one person in their life who has the most experience with an issue. When that happens, it may be appropriate to share direct advice.

5. Help Them Identify the First Actionable Step

A useful last step is to have the child clarify where they will begin. This is critical because it is easy to feel overwhelmed by choices in a situation where there are three or more obstacles, with each having multiple potential solutions. So if they don't learn to identify a clear starting point, they may give up even before they truly begin.

There are three easy ways to identify a good starting point. First, you can ask them to choose the easiest obstacle. The idea is to identify a relatively small step that they can quickly take to build a bit of positive momentum that can carry them through other, more challenging obstacles. This approach tends to be best for younger children who don't yet have the motivation or confidence to start with something a little more challenging.

Second, you can ask them to identify the most *exciting* obstacle. This is a great option for kids of all ages because it leverages their natural interest and enthusiasm. As with the previous step, it can help create a strong sense of momentum that carries them through to their ultimate goal.

Finally, you can ask them to identify the most *uncertain* obstacle. While this is more challenging, it's especially useful in situations where it's unclear whether taking *any* steps are worth it. This approach is common in business startups because there is little point in tackling predictable tasks—coming up with a business name, creating a logo, building a website—if you aren't yet sure that your product idea can be built or will appeal to customers. In such a case, it's smarter to address the greatest area of uncertainty first by validating the product idea.

Obviously, this last option takes more up-front effort and may discourage younger children, so I only recommend it for older kids who are committed to following through on the goal in question.

Here are some examples of prompts that you can use for this final step:

- *What do you see as the best place to begin? Why?*
- *Which of the obstacles do you think will be easiest to solve?*
- *Where are you most excited to begin?*
- *Which of the possible solutions do you want to try first? Then what?*
- *What step is most critical to finding out if your goal is achievable?*
- *Is there an obstacle that is more important than the others?*

If you get a vague or non-actionable response to your set of questions, consider follow-up prompts, such as: "How will you know when you've finished that part?" or "What is involved in completing that?"

Avoid Common Mistakes That Can Sabotage the Process

While there are no hard-and-fast rules when it comes to using this question-guided approach to solve problems, there are some common mistakes adults make. Here are five things to avoid.

Mistake 1 – Using Pseudo-Questions to Assert Opinions

We must catch ourselves when we're tempted to offer up *pseudo-questions*. As described by the Canadian philosopher Charles Taylor, these are assertions or opinions that masquerade as questions. For example, it may be tempting to say something like, "You don't really want to go to that after-school program, do you?" or "The right solution is probably to put in an extra hour of homework each night, right?"

While these are *technically* questions, they are really just transparent attempts to steer the conversation in a specific direction. They present a strong opinion or perspective instead of creating an opportunity for the child to share their thoughts or come up with a solution on their own. When you're tempted to use such questions, remind yourself to use open-ended questions instead.

Mistake 2 – Being Quick to Fill an Awkward Silence

As social creatures, we often feel uncomfortable during small gaps in conversation. When a child takes a few moments to silently think about their response, we may feel the need to jump in to rephrase a question or even hint at possible answers. Yet, doing so is almost always a big mistake.

First, it robs them of the opportunity to carefully consider their response. Second, it can slowly train them to expect us to jump in and help whenever they hesitate, creating a convenient way to have us solve the problem on their behalf. And finally, it can signal to them that we prefer instant answers over thoughtful deliberation.

It's critical that we view silence as evidence that they're thinking deeply. If it turns out they are confused or need clarification, they always have the option to let us know in due time. Rather than immediately filling the awkward void, we must give them time to think and respond at their own pace.

Mistake 3 – Relying Entirely on Fully Formed Questions

You may have noticed that some of the prompts I provided earlier were not complete questions. That's because, in situations where we just want a few more details, it's often a mistake to follow up with an entirely new question. Instead, a few simple prompts like "Tell me more about that" or "And what else?" can work like magic in getting a child to provide far more detail.

One of the advantages of shorter prompts is that they tend to feel more casual and conversational. In contrast, when we focus too much on using complete questions, the process can feel more like an interrogation. So I encourage you to make ample use of shorter questions and prompts.

Mistake 4 – Preventing Kids from Exploring a Known Dead End

It's often tempting to steer our kids away from ideas or strategies that we know won't work out. After all, wouldn't their time be better spent on strategies that have a chance of leading to success? Won't doing so help them make faster progress and avoid unnecessary frustration? Not quite. In fact, one of the very best ways for a child to develop their problem-solving abilities is by learning from their own mistakes.

Pointing out to a child that an idea won't work is no substitute for having them discover it on their own. It's only by trying things for themselves that they can pick up on the subtle nuances of what went right, what went wrong, and what they might do differently when facing a similar situation in the future.

Mistake 5 – Assuming You Know the Best Solution

Much of the wisdom we accumulate over our lives translates to a better understanding of our unique strengths and preferences. In effect, we get better and better at making choices that are optimized for how *we* think and how *we* experience the world. The downside is that this can lead us to mistakenly assume what's best for us is also best for others, including our children.

If we aren't careful, our biases can start to creep into the problem-solving process, and we can start guiding our children toward outcomes that don't align with their needs. Consequently, it's critical to remind ourselves that we don't really know what it's like to be them or what they care about most. So, again, instead of pushing conversations in a specific direction, we should use open-ended questions to let our kids reach their own conclusions.

Help Kids Learn How to Ask Effective Questions

Our objective is to prepare our kids to solve problems without the need for our assistance. Ultimately, then, they will have to learn how to ask effective questions on their own. With this in mind, we must guide their problem-solving development through three key stages.

Stage 1 – Model the Use of Effective Questions

In this first stage, we are simply helping our children work through problems and challenges using the five steps we covered earlier, each with their own questions and prompts. Doing so helps familiarize them with the fundamentals of problem solving so they can learn how to identify the core of an issue, break down challenges into manageable chunks, and brainstorm potential solutions. In effect, we are *modeling* an approach to problem solving that they can later use on their own.

Stage 2 – Invite Them to Pose Questions for Others

As our kids become more comfortable with problem solving, we can look for opportunities to involve them in asking questions when others are stuck. For example, if someone they know—a friend, sibling, or even a fictional character in a story—is facing a challenge, you might ask them, "What questions do you think will make it easier for them to find a solution?" Or, alternatively, you can invite them to help guide *you* through resolving a difficulty you're facing (assuming it's age-appropriate, of course).

The goal of this second stage is to help your child recognize that they, too, can pose useful questions or prompts—and to give them a chance to practice doing it. If their initial attempts miss the mark, avoid correcting or rejecting their ideas. Instead, simply add in a few suggestions of your own to further model the kinds of questions that are most helpful.

Stage 3 – Set Them Up to Ask Questions of Themselves

The final stage is helping our kids learn to tackle their own challenges. This tends to be more difficult than guiding others because we're often less objective about solving our own problems. It's much simpler to offer advice from the outside. So, while practicing the problem-solving process with others in stage 2 is helpful, it won't fully prepare a child for the complexities of handling their own issues.

An effective way to help them view things more objectively is to ask a meta-question, such as: "What would you ask or advise a friend if they were facing this challenge?"

While it may seem basic, this question is based on one of my favorite insights from the 2021 book *Chatter*, by psychologist and neuroscientist Ethan Kross. The prompt is uniquely powerful because it creates what Kross describes as *mental distance*: the ability to view a situation from a less emotional and more objective perspective. By inquiring "What would you ask or advise a friend?" we can set a child up to view a personal challenge as if it were happening to someone else. This, in turn, makes it far easier for them to focus on the resolution process and see the truth of the matter, rather than getting swept up in emotion.

Speaking of mental shifts: The key to working through these three stages is changing how we view our role as parents. If we believe we're responsible for delivering an easy, predictable, or carefree life for our children, then it can feel incredibly rewarding to step in and resolve problems on their behalf. However, if we can appreciate that they're better served by learning how to confidently take on life's challenges *on their own*, it becomes far more rewarding to measure our success as parents based on how their problem-solving skills are developing over time.

Taking Action on Principle 5

Nurture problem solving with open-ended questions. Rather than offering direct advice or stepping in to solve challenges on a child's behalf, we can use simple but effective prompts to help them develop their own problem-solving abilities. Here are five tips to help you get started:

1. **Start by digging deeper into the problem and their attempts to resolve it.** The first step in working toward a solution is understanding what a child has tried, where they got stuck, and how they're viewing the challenge at hand. Not only is this helpful in guiding them toward a solution, but it also helps identify potential weaknesses or gaps in their problem-solving abilities.
2. **Guide them through the problem-solving framework.** Once you have a sense of the problem they are facing, it's

time to use open-ended questions to help them clarify the core issue, identify key obstacles, and brainstorm potential solutions.
3. **Help them choose the first actionable step.** Children often feel stuck due to a sense of overwhelm. So even after helping them identify a list of potential solutions, it's crucial to have them clarify where they will begin.
4. **Invite them to come up with questions to help others.** As our kids become more comfortable with the problem-solving process, it's helpful to provide them with opportunities to apply it. And one of the very best ways to do that is to have them suggest questions when others are stuck.
5. **As they become more familiar with effective problem solving, give them opportunities to resolve challenges on their own.** The difference here is that you won't be asking all the questions. Instead, you'll monitor them as they ask and answer things on their own. A powerful way to get them started is by asking: "What would you ask or advise a friend if they were facing this challenge?"

A great way to reward a child's problem-solving efforts (and reinforce other useful behaviors) is through the use of praise. Unfortunately, not all forms of praise are equal and some can be downright harmful so it's important that we learn the difference. That is the focus of the next chapter.

PRINCIPLE 6

Reinforce Kids' Growth with Detailed Praise

Few things inspire parents to lay on the praise as quickly as a display of intellectual skill. "You're so smart!" and "You're such a fast learner" are undoubtedly two of the most popular compliments bestowed on kids. There's a problem, though: These forms of praise don't really help. And they can actually hold kids back.

You may be wondering, "What could possibly be wrong with telling a child they're smart? Isn't it a great way to let them know they can accomplish anything? And what's wrong with praising them for learning quickly? Isn't it helpful to reward success?"

Not always, as it turns out. In this chapter, we'll explore what can go wrong with this kind of well-intentioned praise. And then we'll discuss a much better way to encourage children to help them achieve their full potential.

The good news is that we don't have to avoid offering praise entirely. We simply need to use it in a way that is more effective for supporting a child's growth.

Praising Intelligence and Speed Creates Harmful Incentives

As human beings, we are wired to seek the approval and admiration of others, especially those we look up to or who are close to us. As a result, children are more likely to repeat actions or behaviors that elicit praise from the influential people in their life. More often than not this is a good thing, but sometimes praise can backfire by creating incentives that hinder development.

For an explanation, let's take a closer look at the two examples we just discussed.

1. Labeling a Child as Smart, Brilliant, or Gifted

When a child is repeatedly praised for being "smart," the label can become a key part of their self-image and social identity. When this happens, they can become incentivized to take fewer risks, develop a greater fear of failure, ask fewer questions, avoid difficult challenges, and—in some cases—even cheat to meet expectations. In short, they can be driven to protect their status of being considered "smart," and thus avoid actions that might call it into question.

Rather than pursuing difficult challenges that can create new opportunities for growth, they tend to play it safe by choosing easier goals or sticking with things that take advantage of their existing abilities. They're less likely to subject themselves to new struggles and difficulties, even if doing so would help them gain new knowledge or skills.

2. Praising a Child for Achieving Quick or Easy Results

Children who are praised for the *speed* or *ease* with which they learn often fall into a similar trap. In an effort to protect their image as a "quick learner," they tend to play it safe by selecting easier goals and avoiding the kinds of challenges that might require more time or effort. Once again, this limits their opportunities for further growth and development.

To make matters worse, such children can start to view learning speed as being predictive of their potential in a given area. This is especially true when a parent or role model links the idea of learning speed with intelligence by saying something like, "You're so smart; you learned that very quickly!" While this can be encouraging whenever they get off to a strong start, it can backfire by causing them to second-guess their abilities in situations where they initially struggle. The result? They may give up prematurely on activities they'd end up loving or being good at.

Positive Labels Place an Unhealthy Focus on Innate Ability

The deeper problem with using labels like "smart," "quick," or even "stupid" is that they describe *fixed traits*. As a result, they nurture the development of a *fixed mindset*, as described by psychologist Carol S. Dweck in her popular book *Mindset*. When this happens, kids start to consider their abilities as being largely predetermined. In other words, they assume their capacity for growth in certain areas—such as math, science, creative writing, sports, or music—is hardwired. They start to believe that they either have the natural ability to succeed in one or more of these areas, or they don't.

When we use fixed labels to encourage our children, we inadvertently fix the way they assess their potential. On one hand, they start to identify areas in which they've received praise and seem to do well relative to their peers, perhaps due to some innate strengths or the support of a great teacher. On the other hand, they begin to focus less on areas where they clearly struggle relative to others, and for which they receive little or no sincere praise.

The contrast between these two types of experiences can lead to the formation of *self-limiting beliefs*, where a child starts to view themselves as being incapable of achieving success in certain areas. After all, if learning quickly is associated with being *smart* or *talented*, what should a child assume about their abilities in areas where their progress is slow or where they initially struggle to keep up with their peers? As Dweck explains, people with a fixed mindset mistakenly conclude, "If at first you don't succeed, you probably don't have the ability."[15]

People with a *growth mindset* also believe they begin life with strengths and weaknesses. However, they view this as only their starting point, understanding that effort and perseverance can also determine whether or not they ultimately succeed. They still experience difficulties and setbacks, but rather than feeling permanently stuck, they view them as obstacles that can be overcome.

This difference in attitude is so powerful because failure is a normal, even desirable aspect of life. If we're never failing, then we're never pushing ourselves to take on difficult challenges or learn new things.

Children with a fixed mindset are more likely to view temporary failure as a permanent judgment of their abilities. If something doesn't come quickly or easily, they're likely to conclude that they lack the natural talent to succeed in that area. As a result, they often quit things they would otherwise enjoy simply because they don't think they can do well, or they want to avoid drawing attention to their perceived shortcomings.

Both mindsets tend to be self-fulfilling. If a child concludes that they lack the natural talent to succeed in a given area, they're less likely to invest the time and effort required to excel, so they end up getting exactly what their (fixed) mindset expects. Likewise, if they believe they can learn something challenging, they will be more inclined to devote time and effort to doing so, thus achieving what their (growth) mindset expects. As Henry Ford famously said, "Whether you think you can, or you think you can't, you're right."

It's worth noting that each one of us tends to maintain a blend of both mindsets. So a child may have a growth mindset when it comes to activities in which they've found some past success. Yet, at the very same time, they may exhibit the traits of a fixed mindset when it comes to areas in which they've started to form self-limiting beliefs.

Now, some might argue that self-limiting beliefs are just a normal part of life. After all, we hope our children will lean into the activities that come naturally to them or that they most enjoy, as covered in principle 2. So perhaps it's acceptable if certain types of praise unintentionally hamper progress in other areas. The real issue, though, is that we can't predict which skills our children will want to develop in the future—or how the self-limiting beliefs they're forming today might keep them from pursuing those skills down the road.

By way of example, for most of my life I've had a self-limiting belief around public speaking. I don't recall at what age it began, but I can remember a few situations where I felt very uncomfortable in front of a live audience. And, when I would see others speak with greater confidence, I assumed they had a natural ability that I lacked. As a result, I started to avoid situations that I now realize would have allowed me to develop this valuable skill. Later in life, I missed out on many opportunities in both my personal and professional life due to my lack of confidence in this area.

Of course, I'm not unique in having such an experience. I've come across many people whose lives have been hindered by self-limiting beliefs of one kind or another. Often these relate to skills they sincerely wish they could develop. Perhaps they've dreamed of playing an instrument, creating hand-drawn artwork, or coding a smartphone application. Yet, for one reason or another, they've concluded that such possibilities are out of reach due to a few experiences that left them with the impression that they don't have what it takes to pursue them successfully.

Our praise for our children doesn't have to plant the seeds of self-limiting beliefs. We can encourage them in ways that highlight their strengths while simultaneously helping them appreciate that they have what it takes to pursue any skill or ability, whether or not it seems to come naturally to them.

Before we get into the details, though, first let's explore why the idea of "natural talent" is overrated—and how this relates to our children's capacity for growth.

Mental Representations Matter More Than Natural Talent

It's easy to fixate on minor differences in initial ability. Yet, the truth is that each one of us has the potential to develop remarkable skills and knowledge. Nobody is born with the ability to speak a language, ride a bike, or read a book. But not only can we learn these kinds of highly complex skills, we can master them to the point that they feel almost automatic. And yet, even knowing this, we tend to greatly overestimate the impact of natural talent while simultaneously underestimating the extreme adaptability of the human brain.

Historically, people have assumed that raw intelligence or innate ability were key to one's success. After all, these factors have been shown to be a reliable predictor for early achievement in many pursuits. A great example of this is the game of chess. Beginners who have a higher IQ tend to outperform similarly experienced peers. But here's where things get interesting: Numerous studies suggest that beyond the very early stages of learning the game, superior play is *not* linked with IQ. The value of raw intelligence gets replaced by an awareness of proven strategies for playing the game more effectively. This means that a player of average IQ who has spent a dozen hours studying the game can easily dominate a high-IQ beginner who would otherwise be viewed as having "natural talent" for the game.[16]

Key to expert performance is the development of appropriate *mental representations*, as described by Swedish psychologist K. Anders Ericsson. The concept is similar to the idea of mental models that we first explored in principle 3, but in this case we're talking about models that relate to more specialized skills or knowledge. They make it easier for experienced people to spot patterns, make sense of complexity, and achieve otherwise impossible outcomes in specific areas of expertise.

For example, consider what it takes to become a professional BMX bike rider. Nobody has an innate ability to launch themselves off huge dirt jumps, perform controlled backflips and twists in the air, and land smoothly on two wheels. Instead, they must first develop mental representations relating to balance, coordination, spatial awareness, muscle control, timing, pattern recognition, and much more. Crucially, each of these areas develop progressively as the rider takes on lower-level challenges, such as learning to ride a bike, take a jump, land smoothly, and perform isolated flips or other tricks (perhaps first on a trampoline).

Every complex skill is built on a similar foundation of *mental representations*. Whether someone is setting out to play competitive ice hockey, perform an improvised guitar solo, or write a compelling novel, what matters most is the development of mental representations that allow their brains to avoid being overwhelmed by too much complexity all at once. No amount of raw intelligence or natural talent can overcome this need. Simply put, the brain requires purposeful practice to automate or systematize many of the sub-skills required to take on complex activities.

The upshot is that a child who hasn't developed the mental representations needed for certain skills—like math, science, or writing—can find such activities significantly more daunting. Worse still, if they don't have an understanding of the brain's incredible ability to adapt through purposeful practice, they can convince themselves they will never be good at these types of skills.

We'll explore the use and development of mental representations more in the next chapter, but the key takeaway here is that every child has the potential to learn far more than they tend to give themselves credit for. Our role as parents, then, is to ensure they take advantage of this potential by helping them develop and maintain a growth mindset. The goal isn't to have them attempt to master every skill they encounter, but to approach any challenge with the confidence that they can learn most things—so long as they are willing to invest the appropriate amount of time and effort.

How to Help Children Develop and Maintain a Growth Mindset

Given how incredibly common fixed thinking is today (across all age groups), we shouldn't be surprised that so many children adopt this view. For many of us, the myth of fixed ability is simply assumed; it's almost subconscious. Fortunately, there are simple things we can do to help kids develop and maintain a growth mindset. Here are four of them.

1. Point to Examples of Easy Things That Were Once Difficult

At its core, a growth mindset is about recognizing that anyone can improve their abilities. One of the fastest ways to help a child escape fixed thinking, then, is to point to the times when *they* overcame difficulty. For example, we can remind them how challenging it was for them to learn how to ride a bike, and then point out how easy and automatic it is for them now.

The key is to identify growth moments that were both (a) highly challenging and (b) recent enough for them to remember in vivid detail. So if riding a bike was something that came easily for them or occurred too long ago, you can choose another event. Any parent will have countless examples to draw from, such as when they first learned to walk, run, skate, read, write, type, draw, shoot a basketball, hit a baseball, do multiplication, solve a Rubik's Cube, play an instrument, and on and on.

If they have younger siblings or cousins who are actively pursuing skills they've already mastered, you can ask them to observe the younger child's learning process. This can be a powerful way to help them appreciate the stark transition from struggle and frustration to ease and confidence.

Personally, I like to drive this lesson home with a simple mantra that I often repeat with my kids: "Hard things become easy with practice." I reference it when they're frustrated with a new challenge, when they see someone struggling with a skill they've already mastered, and when they witness others doing impressive things with apparent ease. It's a great way to remind them that almost everything worth learning is frustrating or difficult in the beginning but, with practice, eventually becomes easy and relatively automatic.

2. Provide Context for Other People's Success and Progress

Perhaps the most common reason why kids buy into the hype of natural talent is that they routinely witness the impressive abilities of others without having a chance to appreciate the journey or backstory. This extends beyond simply seeing world-class musicians, athletes, or artists showing off their impressive abilities. The same issue can crop up when a child witnesses a friend, sibling, or classmate appearing to learn something more quickly or more easily than them.

Of course, some kids will simply pick up certain skills faster than others, which can be discouraging to those who find themselves progressing more slowly. In these situations, it can be useful to point out that innate advantages tend to be limited to the early stages of a pursuit, as we covered earlier. Better yet, we can help them appreciate other, controllable factors that may be at play.

For instance, a child may be learning faster due to better learning strategies, spending more time practicing, having a better teacher, or transferring skills they've gained from another, similar activity. By bringing these possibilities to our children's attention, we not only help them make sense of others' seemingly rapid progress, we also help them identify ways to boost their own progress. (More on this in the next chapter.)

3. When Children Struggle or Fail, Encourage Them to Try *Differently*

Every child encounters challenges that cause them to experience frustration or even outright failure. When this happens, parents and teachers tend to offer advice that emphasizes the value of *perseverance*. While this can be helpful, it can also be misinterpreted as urging them to simply try harder or stick with the problem for longer.

The notion that a child should *try harder* can be disheartening if, from their perspective, they're already giving 100 percent of their effort. As a result, they may start to slip into a fixed mindset. After all, if they're already trying their best and aren't having success, they may conclude they lack the natural ability to succeed. And, if they interpret the advice to mean they should *stick with the problem for longer*, they may end up wasting a lot of time and energy repeating the approach that led to failure in the first place.

"Generally the solution is not 'try harder' but rather 'try differently,'" according to K. Anders Ericsson and his coauthor, Robert Pool, in *Peak*.[17] So when it comes to helping a child persevere, we must also encourage them to explore entirely new approaches. A great way to communicate this is by sharing these wise words from Dweck: "Everyone learns in a different way. Let's keep trying to find the way that works for you."[18]

For example, if a child is struggling to learn words or phrases in a new language using a smartphone app, you might encourage them to try flashcards instead. Or if they can't bring themselves to commit to trying a backflip on a trampoline, you might suggest they try it off the edge of a diving board instead, so they can land safely in water.

The core insight here is that we are all different. Each one of us has distinct strengths, backgrounds, and existing mental representations. While there may be a "best practice" for learning a specific skill or overcoming a certain challenge, we need to keep in mind that the common approach may not be right for our child. When they are struggling, rather than just recommending that they persevere, encourage them to try alternative methods.

4. Replace Quick and Easy Results with Meaningful Challenges

Another powerful way to help kids achieve their full potential is to replace the appeal of quick and easy results with the joy and satisfaction that comes from taking on difficult challenges.

This begins with changing the way we react to the speed or ease with which they learn something new. For instance, if a child is quick to complete an exercise or challenge, rather than praising their intelligence or speed we can take Dweck's advice and say something like, "Sorry, I guess that was too easy. Let's find something more challenging, so you can continue to learn and grow."

As your children grow older, you can build on this philosophy by setting the expectation that everyone in the family should be taking on at least one difficult challenge at any given time—adults included. The dinner table is a great place to facilitate this. During your evening conversations, you can go around the table and have everyone share one hard skill, problem, or goal they are currently working on or plan to start tackling. Everyone gets to select their own challenges, but they are expected to share regular updates with the family.

A child might choose to highlight a difficult task from school, such as preparing for a major exam. Alternatively, they may be working on something that can be done in their free time, such as learning to solve a Rubik's Cube, spin a basketball on their finger, or develop another skill. For a parent, it might involve picking up a new hobby, building a new habit, or developing a skill at work. The idea is to establish a culture of continuous learning. In doing this, we shift our family's value system away from prioritizing speed and ease and toward an appreciation of taking on genuine challenges.

As parents, we can also use these conversations as an opportunity to normalize what it's really like to take on something difficult. You might share an update on your own project by saying, "I have no idea how I'm going to solve this one, because my first two attempts didn't work." Then, modeling a growth mindset, you might add, "...but I know it's possible, so I just have to find the approach that will work best for me."

Praise Actions and Behaviors That Support Continued Growth

Praise is most effective when it's used to reinforce positive *behavior*, not positive *results*. So when it comes to encouraging our children, it's best to direct our praise toward efforts, actions, or processes that contributed to successful outcomes. In other words, rather than praising fixed traits or even direct achievements, praise the specific things that led to them.

Here are four simple tips that highlight how this works.

Tip 1 – Wait for success, *then* praise useful actions.

One of the most common mistakes parents make after learning about the growth mindset is to praise any and all effort from their children to encourage them to start taking action. In some cases, they even praise when no effort is being made at all. While this encouragement is understandable, keep in mind that praise should be a tool for reinforcing existing behavior, not initiating it.

It's crucial, then, that we save our praise until our child achieves a meaningful outcome. Once that happens, we should focus our praise on the actions that led to it. So, for example, instead of saying "You're smart" or "I'm proud of you for getting an A+ on the test," we might say, "You studied hard for that test and it paid off!" or "You put in the time and effort to do well and it shows!"

The same approach can be used to reinforce *any* action or behavior that has contributed to a successful outcome. If a child's sense of curiosity or their willingness to explore diverse interests leads to an interesting breakthrough, we can reinforce this behavior by saying something like, "I love how you're always trying new things!" or "It's great to see you exploring new hobbies and coming up with new ideas!"

Meanwhile, in situations where a child's effort is failing to produce a result, we can subtly encourage them while redirecting their focus toward finding a solution that works. In these situations, we can once again take Dweck's advice and say something like, "I like the effort you put in, but it looks like that method didn't work. Let's try another way."

Tip 2 – Make your praise as specific as possible.

Praise is most useful when it's specific and detailed. The more precise we are with our praise the easier it is for our children to identify and repeat useful behaviors. Better still, by highlighting specific things they're doing well, we show that we're paying attention and that we care about the small details that contribute to their success. So, if a child plays a particularly good game of basketball or hockey, rather than offering up generic praise like "Great job out there. You played well!" we might instead say, "I like the way you were getting open and making it easier for teammates to pass to you" or "I like how you focused on being in the right position to score."

If a child completes a lengthy homework assignment, instead of saying "That was a lot of work. Great job!" you might say, "That was a big assignment, and I admire how you were able to stay focused and avoid distractions until you finished!"

If they tackle a particularly difficult or complex challenge, instead of saying "Great job finding a solution," you might say, "I like the way you tried several strategies, and I admire how you kept at it until you found the one that worked best."

Providing this kind of detail can be dramatically more effective than generic praise. If you're anything like me, you can probably recall a few times in your life when people praised you in such a specific way and, crucially, how that praise made you feel. Odds are that you not only were more likely to repeat the behavior, but that you sought to do even better the next time.

Tip 3 – Target remarkable or outstanding behavior.

As with so many good things in life, praise is most effective in moderation. While we don't want to hold back when it comes to encouraging our children, jumping on every minor opportunity to heap on praise can water down its impact. It's most useful to focus our praise on truly remarkable or outstanding behavior.

The goalposts for this will naturally shift over the course of a child's life. In their earlier years, it's okay to be more liberal with our praise, since much of what they accomplish will be for the very first time and we want to reinforce new positive behaviors. However, as they grow older, it's essential to be more selective with our praise so it doesn't lose its power.

Tip 4 – If you're going to use labels, choose active labels.

It's generally best to avoid using labels such as "smart," "clever," or "gifted." But some labels can be useful if they're paired with detailed praise. I call these *active labels* because they describe patterns of behavior rather than fixed traits. For example, you might label a child as being "organized," "determined," "curious," "creative," "inquisitive," "optimistic," or "loyal."

One great way to use these kinds of labels is through a simple three-step process developed by parent educators Adele Faber and Elaine Mazlish. In their popular book *How to Talk So Kids Will Listen & Listen So Kids Will Talk*, they recommend (1) describing what you see, (2) describing how it makes you feel, and (3) reinforcing the child's praiseworthy behavior with a single keyword that can serve as a positive label.

For example, if you've noticed that a child has tidied up their bedroom, you might say, "I see a clean floor, a well-made bed, and toys that are all put away." Then you might describe how this makes you feel by adding, "It feels great to walk into this tidy room." Finally, you might sum everything up and make use of an active label by saying, "You sorted your Legos, books, and drawings and put them where they belong. That's what I call being *organized*!"

Notice how this approach doesn't involve labeling them with a fixed trait. Instead of making a definitive claim ("You're an organized person" or "You're so organized"), we describe the way they are acting by saying they are "being organized." It's a subtle difference, but one that places greater emphasis on the desirable behavior that they are exhibiting.

Taking Action on Principle 6

Reinforce kids' growth with detailed praise. By doing so, we make it more likely that our children will develop a growth mindset, continue to take on difficult challenges, and learn valuable lessons along the way. Here are five tips to get started:

1. **Avoid praising a child for raw intelligence or learning speed.** This tends to create the wrong incentives and put an unhealthy focus on innate ability. Worse still, it distracts from more powerful and controllable factors that can help the child achieve their full potential in life.
2. **Foster a growth mindset by highlighting skills that were once difficult.** Nobody is born with the ability to ride a bike, read a book, or even speak a language—yet not only do kids develop these skills, they master them to the point

that they feel almost automatic. Drawing their attention to this fact is a powerful way to remind them that "hard things become easy with practice."

3. **When kids are stuck, encourage them to *try differently*.** There are many ways to learn new skills, overcome setbacks, and acquire knowledge. So when a child is struggling, rather than pushing them to "try harder," help them try *differently* by exploring alternative methods that might be a better fit for them.

4. **Hold your praise until a positive outcome has been achieved.** Praise is a tool for reinforcing behaviors, not initiating them. Thus, it's critical that we wait for our kids to achieve a meaningful outcome before offering praise (while being sure to direct it toward the actions or behaviors that contributed to their success).

5. **Be detailed in the praise you offer.** The more specific and selective we are with our praise, the more impact it can have. Focus on identifying the most useful actions that you want to see repeated in the future, and then offer up targeted and descriptive praise to reinforce them.

Up until this point in the book, we've largely focused on helping kids explore diverse experiences and build flexible knowledge. You may be starting to wonder, then, how to best support them when they decide to narrow their focus and commit to a larger goal or more ambitious pursuit. That's what we'll address in the next chapter.

PRINCIPLE 7

Boost Skill Development with Proven Strategies

In principles 2 and 3, we covered the many benefits of giving children the freedom to explore self-selected hobbies rather than pushing them to specialize too soon.

Eventually, however, as they get older, they'll likely begin to identify a smaller set of pursuits that they want to take more seriously. It's at this point that targeted strategies for mastering skills and knowledge can really make a big difference. So, in this chapter, we're going to cover some of the most useful and impactful techniques for accelerating their pace of learning.

While some of the insights that follow can be applied to a child's casual interests, many of them are better suited to helping them follow through on more ambitious efforts. With that in mind, before taking action, be sure you have a clear sense of what your child wants to achieve so you can guide them toward strategies that are appropriate for their level of commitment.

DINNER TIME CONVERSATIONS

Prioritize Direct Experience Early and Often

When it comes to developing a skill, there are few substitutes for getting direct, real-world experience. For example, if a child wants to play basketball, encourage them to start participating in games at their skill level. If they want to learn to play the guitar, recommend they start playing along to some of their favorite songs as early as possible. If they want to code powerful smartphone applications, encourage them to build simple, functional apps sooner rather than later.

To some, this advice may seem painfully obvious. Yet prioritizing *direct experience* is in stark contrast to the way many things are taught today. Much of what a child learns in the classroom is abstracted away from real-world situations. Students are taught to memorize facts, concepts, and formulas before gaining an appreciation for how they can be used in a practical way. Likewise, skills are often taught in simplified, isolated environments. Sometimes this is necessary, but often it's done to help a child reach learning milestones faster while sacrificing a more holistic approach to education.

This can easily lead a child to follow a similar strategy when it comes time to pursue their own interests. Left to their own devices, a child who wishes to play basketball might choose to practice shooting or dribbling a ball alone in their driveway, thereby avoiding or delaying the challenge of playing in real games. Likewise, someone who wants to play the guitar may spend countless hours practicing chord shapes and scales while avoiding the difficulty of putting them together to play a full song. And a child interested in building smartphone apps might watch endless tutorials on YouTube instead of opening a code editor and struggling through the process of building something basic.

It's easy to see why kids—and adults—do this. As author Scott H. Young explains in his book *Ultralearning*, "Directly learning the thing we want feels too uncomfortable, boring, or frustrating, so we settle for some book, lecture, or app, hoping it will eventually make us better at the real thing."[19]

He goes on to point out that one of the greatest challenges in developing skills or knowledge relates to "transfer," the process by which we learn something in one context, such as shooting a basketball in a driveway, and are able to apply it in another, such as shooting a basketball during a competitive game. The problem is that experience in one context often fails to translate well into another. It's one thing to make shot after shot in a controlled, familiar environment; it's another altogether to take the same shot in a new environment, in the face of a strong defender, after receiving an awkward pass, while also being tired from running up and down the basketball court.

Participating in the goal activity early and often is how children learn to minimize transfer issues. As Young puts it, "If you can spend a good portion of your learning time just doing the thing you want to get better at, the problem [of transfer] will likely go away."[20] Going through this process has two major benefits. First, it makes it easier to identify skills worth practicing. And second, it helps you refine newly acquired skills through direct experience.

This obviously may not be an option for every pursuit. Some activities may be too complex, difficult, or dangerous to dive right into. However, the goal should be to close the gap between isolated practice and real-world experience as soon as it's safe or appropriate. That way, children can learn in a more dynamic environment and avoid falling into the trap of endlessly developing isolated skills that may not transfer effectively.

Ensure Continuous Progress Through Purposeful Practice

One of the most common misconceptions when it comes to personal growth is that spending additional time just *participating* in an activity leads to increased skill or competence. For instance, many people believe that a doctor with twenty years of experience is always superior to one with only five. However, studies have shown that once someone reaches an acceptable level of performance, additional years of experience don't automatically lead to further improvement. If anything, it's more likely that their skill will slowly deteriorate as time passes.[21]

Time spent simply engaging in your work or a hobby is not the same as practicing for improvement. Ericsson calls this kind of casual participation "naive practice." While this approach can help beginners progress, it can only take them so far.

A child setting out to play basketball may develop some of the basics—dribbling, passing, and shooting—by simply playing in casual games. And by continuing to play the game over several weeks or months they may shore up a few obvious weaknesses. Once they grasp the basics, however, there's a strong chance they'll hit a plateau and stop improving, even with additional months or even years of play.

The key to breaking out of such a rut is to engage in what Ericsson defines as "purposeful practice." This involves getting outside our comfort zone to learn specific skills in a focused way, with clear goals, a plan for reaching those goals, and a way to monitor progress along the way. Unlike naive practice, purposeful practice requires clear expectations and deliberate focus; in other words, the quality of the practice matters more than the quantity. The hallmark of it, Ericsson and Pool write in *Peak*, is "that you try to do something you cannot do...and that you practice it over and over again, focusing on exactly how you are doing it, where you are falling short, and how you can get better."[22]

As we covered in the last chapter, the key to performing at a high level is to develop *mental representations* that make it easier to spot patterns, make sense of complexity, and achieve outcomes that are otherwise unlikely or impossible. Even when a skill is primarily physical, proper mental frameworks can have a huge impact on failure or success.

Examples of this process of information encoding are all around us. Almost everything we do, including walking, speaking, reading, and writing is built on a complex web of mental representations. Without them, even the simple act of walking would require that we actively coordinate a complex series of muscle movements, paying close attention to all the minor details each and every time we take a step.

Purposeful practice is a highly efficient way to rewire the brain to make challenging things easier. It initiates a virtuous cycle, because the development of better mental representations makes it easier for someone to monitor and evaluate how well they are doing. Thus, the more skilled someone becomes, the better their mental representations will be, and the better their mental representations are, the more effectively they can further improve their skill.

This is one reason why experts in all fields often appear to be fast learners. Their superior mental representations, developed through years of focused practice, provide a stronger foundation for acquiring related skills, abilities, and knowledge. So, while it may be true that they can learn faster *today*, that wasn't always the case. It's their relevant experience that enables them to improve at a faster rate than those who lack the same mental representations.

All of this is to say that purposeful practice is the key to pushing beyond one's innate abilities. A child who wants to excel at something needs to dedicate time and effort toward acquiring relevant skills or knowledge. In doing so, they can rewire their brain to turn difficult or complex skills into things that are effortless or even automatic. This in turn will make it easier for them to stack or combine related skills to achieve results that would otherwise be impossible.

Before we move on, a quick clarification. If it seems like this sort of dedication and effort is at odds with the casual pursuit of self-selected hobbies covered in principles 2 and 3, you'd be largely right. As I mentioned at the beginning of this chapter, the advice here is most relevant to children who have decided on the activities they want to pursue more deeply. Most likely, these are older children who have had time to explore many different types of pursuits or, at the very least, are choosing (on their own) to explore something more deeply.

Accelerate Learning with the Direct-Then-Drill Approach

You may have noticed that I started this chapter by touting the value of *direct experience* and then switched gears to highlight the value of *purposeful practice*. The former involves participating in the goal activity while the latter involves improving skills through focused, isolated practice. The reason for this is that the two methods are most effective when used in combination. Young refers to this as the "direct-then-drill" approach.

Direct participation provides a foundation for learning fundamentals and gaining practical experience. Then, once someone identifies a weakness or opportunity for improvement, they can use purposeful practice to isolate and drill relevant skills. Critically, the resulting improvements can then be integrated back into the activity so they, too, can be refined as needed.

For example, a child interested in playing chess should start participating in real games as soon as possible. In doing so, they will begin to identify shortcomings that can most effectively be addressed through purposeful practice. This knowledge is then used to decide how they will spend their practice time to shore up relevant skills—learning stronger opening gambits, improving middlegame strategy, etc. At every step along the way, it's critical that they integrate what they have learned back into the games they are playing. That way they can gain experience using their improved skills and continue to get a refined sense of what to work on next.

This approach can be challenging and uncomfortable at times. As a result, some children may insist on delaying direct experience in favor of doubling down on isolated practice. Remember, though, that participating in the goal activity is the only way they can be sure they're refining the right skills in the right order. Without this approach, it's all too easy to spend countless hours on things that either fail to transfer to the goal activity or are simply unnecessary.

The direct-then-drill approach can be applied to almost any pursuit, whether it's starting a business, writing a book, or learning an instrument. In each case, it starts with finding the most direct way to participate in the goal activity. Then, as setbacks or challenges arise, time is set aside to engage in purposeful practice to develop relevant skills or knowledge. Along the way, new skills and knowledge are integrated back into the goal activity so they can be refined through direct experience.

Create Opportunities for Gathering Actionable Feedback

Regardless of what a child is learning or how they're learning it, feedback plays a critical role in accelerating their progress. It can make all the difference when it comes to catching mistakes early, adopting (or bypassing) best practices, and avoiding stalled growth. Therefore, it's essential to create conditions where a child's progress is routinely observed by a qualified teacher, mentor, or coach who can provide actionable feedback.

Of course, not all feedback is useful or productive. As we explored in the previous chapter, anything that promotes a fixed mindset or places undue emphasis on innate ability runs the risk of stalling or reversing progress.

The best feedback addresses current mistakes and guides future action. This kind of feedback should describe what the child is doing wrong and how to fix it, or what the child is doing right and how to refine things further. Importantly, it should address the *performance* rather than the person. Generally, this requires a qualified coach or teacher who has deep subject matter expertise, plus a history of successfully guiding others through the same learning process.

Direct experience alone can provide some limited feedback. As mentioned earlier, a child playing basketball for the first time will start to identify skills and abilities that are fundamental to the sport and, as a result, begin to develop a sense of what they need to improve. However, external feedback from a qualified coach will allow for much more rapid advancement. So once a child is serious about making progress toward a specific goal, it's best to put them in situations where they can receive this kind of feedback on a regular basis. This might involve scheduling private lessons, group sessions, or other activities that are monitored by qualified instructors.

Beyond simple correct feedback, another powerful resource is what Young calls "meta-feedback," which he describes as feedback that "isn't about your performance but about evaluating the overall success of the strategy you're using to learn."[23] Rather than identifying specific mistakes that a child may be making, this feedback addresses the approach they're using to acquire new skills. For example, learning a new language using an interactive smartphone app may be inferior to going to a meetup where you can practice talking with native speakers. (If it's not practical to go to regular meetups, there may still be other tools that are more useful than an app, such as flashcards.)

Naturally, there will be situations where it's impossible to find subject matter experts. Some emerging hobbies or interests may be so new, or so obscure, that qualified teachers or coaches don't exist (at least not in a way that's convenient). In such situations, it can still be beneficial to gather external feedback from non-experts, including parents. That's because, as a general rule, it's easier for outside observers (expert and non-expert alike) to accurately assess mistakes. In fact, a child who captures their own actions on video, and later views them as an outside observer, is better able to identify their own mistakes. (With all of this in mind, non-experts' suggestions for fixing mistakes should always be taken with a grain of salt, as it's easier for them to identify issues than to come up with corrective advice.)

Encourage a Deeper Understanding of the Fundamentals

Another key to effective learning is taking the time to really understand the fundamentals. This requires digging beneath best practices and surface knowledge to better understand *why* things work the way they do. When a child truly understands something on a deep level, they're able to transfer their knowledge more flexibly, recall details with greater accuracy, and learn related concepts faster.

Consider the difference between memorizing complex directions to a few specific locations in a new city versus truly knowing the lay of the land. When someone has deep knowledge about a city, they don't have to memorize turn-by-turn directions for every new destination they want to visit. Instead, they're able to recall relevant landmarks, relate new destinations to those landmarks, and thus build a more complete and flexible mental map of the area.

This is yet another reason why children should be encouraged to pursue activities based on genuine interest. When they have a sincere desire to explore something, they're far more likely to put in the time and effort to understand core ideas and concepts. In contrast, when they're forced to learn something, they are more likely to settle for surface knowledge that has limited use in the real world.

In my experience, many people in the white-collar workforce rely too heavily on processes they don't truly understand. As a result, even minor alterations to their workflow can be a cause for panic because they lack the deep knowledge required to adapt on the fly. To make matters worse, much of their supposed "experience" isn't transferable to a new job because it's built on simple routines and protocols rather than a deep understanding of how things *really* work.

To be clear, it's perfectly okay for a child to adopt and follow best practices, especially when they're first starting to explore a new area of interest. But as their knowledge and passion deepens they should avoid relying on processes or formulas as a crutch. Instead, they should seek to understand how things really work and why best practices were established in the first place. Not only can this help them identify when a process is flawed or outdated, but it can also help them understand when it makes sense to break from the rules and improvise to create superior results.

One way we can inspire our children to dig deeper is to challenge them with questions about process. We might ask things like: "Why are things done that way? Do you think that's still the best approach? What else have you tried? How were things done in the past? Have you tried any other methods for achieving the same result? Why or why not?"

Don't demand or insist that they assess everything right away. After all, at any given moment, they may be focused on other aspects of the activity. But by asking more probing questions from time to time, we can plant seeds of curiosity that will eventually inspire them to examine their assumptions, if not today, in the years to come.

Promote Strategies That Boost Long-Term Retention

We've all experienced the frustration of trying to recall something only to come up blank. Unfortunately, the human brain is not wired to retain everything we learn or encounter. Instead, it's optimized to be highly energy efficient so that it can function well even when we have limited access to food—a scenario that was all too common for our ancestors.

Fortunately, there are things we can do to improve our capacity to recall things that matter to us. Our children can use these same techniques to help them retain skills and knowledge as they progress in their hobbies. Let's explore three of the most powerful techniques.

1. Regularly Revisit Essential Information

Every time we revisit something in our minds—whether it's an experience, insight, or skill—we signal to the brain that it's worth remembering. The brain then responds by creating a stronger mental connection to these things. The more often we call up these connections, the stronger they become, making it easier and easier to revisit them in the future.

With this in mind, one simple way for a child to enhance their long-term memory is to space out learning sessions over time. For example, instead of having them practice guitar for five hours on a Sunday, they'd be better off practicing for one hour each weekday. The amount of time spent is the same, but spreading things out helps create stronger mental connections.

Likewise, instead of repeating the same exercise for an entire practice session, it's better to mix things up every few minutes—an approach known as *interleaving*. To continue with our guitar example, instead of just working through one guitar drill over and over again—and allowing short-term memory to carry the session—they can alternate between several distinct areas of practice, such as chords, scales, and learning a new song. While this can sometimes be more mentally exhausting, it greatly enhances recall by creating more opportunities to reinforce long-term memory.

2. Create Strong Connections Between Related Ideas

One of the benefits of deep learning is that it creates stronger and more distributed mental connections. As we covered earlier, it's so much easier to memorize directions to a few new locations in a city when you already have a strong mental map of the area. With this map in place, locations don't have to be stored in isolation; instead, they can be built upon a web of existing mental connections. As a result, not only is it easier to take in and store new information, but the entire mental map is strengthened. It's a self-reinforcing process.

Every time a child learns several related concepts, or connects two or more ideas, they enhance their ability to recall all related information. This is why it's so crucial that we encourage our children to develop a deep understanding of the fundamentals when it comes to their key interests. It's also why it can be so beneficial to build a mental toolbox full of flexible mental models that can be applied across domains. Doing so creates connections between memories or insights that might otherwise be isolated.

For instance, every time a child finds a way to use a mental model like inversion (as first covered in principle 3), they have a chance to revisit and reinforce the times they applied it to other problems. Better still, they will begin to create connections between such experiences. And, the more they use a given mental model, the more likely it is that they will think to use it in future situations.

3. Practice Free Recall Before Reviewing Notes or Answers

Another powerful way to improve retention is by practicing free recall. This involves actively trying to remember the details of something without looking up the answer or being offered any hints or clues. Ideally this should be practiced a while after first learning or encountering the relevant information, so that it's no longer stored in short-term memory.

Here's what this looks like: Say a child recently learned about the concept of SMART goals and is attempting to recall what they learned. Instead of immediately reviewing their notes to remind themselves that the acronym stands for Specific, Measurable, Achievable, Relevant, and Time-Bound, they might instead begin with a session of free recall. This would involve spending a few moments focusing intently on trying to remember as much as possible. During the process, they might remember the "M" stands for *measurable* and that the "T" stands for either *timely* or *time-bound*. They might then ponder what the "S" stands for, and, even if the answer doesn't immediately come to mind, may choose to spend a few minutes thinking of goal-related concepts that might begin with that letter.

Interestingly, even when a child fails to recall critical details, simply engaging in the exercise can enhance their ability to retain the information when they later review their notes.[24] It's as if by practicing free recall they're sending a signal to their brain saying, "I really want to remember this information, so next time I come across it be sure to hold onto it for longer!"

Every Pursuit Offers a Chance to Become a Better Learner

Learning is a skill like any other. In practice, that means every new skill a child acquires enhances their overall ability to learn future skills. Each learning experience helps them refine their understanding of the tools and tactics that work best in various situations. Over time, their mental toolbox will grow to contain many useful learning strategies, including some we covered in this chapter, such as the value of direct experience, purposeful practice, and useful feedback.

As they progress, they will also gain a deeper understanding of common mental models beyond inversion, such as anchoring, confirmation bias, loss aversion, and second-order effects. Eventually, they will come to appreciate how such models can be transferred from one context to another, as covered in principle 3.

Asking effective questions, which we covered at length in principle 5, is a powerful way to help a child capitalize on their experience. The right type of questions can prompt them to reflect on an obstacle in a way that drives them toward a solution. For example, when they are facing a difficult challenge, rather than asking "Do you have any ideas for solving this?," you might instead ask, "Have you solved something like this before?" or "Can you remember facing a similar challenge in the past?"

For younger kids, it can be beneficial to use prompts that are even more direct. You might point out a specific experience from their past that feels similar to the problem or challenge they are facing. Then you might ask a follow-up question like, "Do you remember what worked in that situation?" or "Are there any lessons from that experience that might apply here?"

If this is starting to feel a little overwhelming, just remember that *life is a long journey*. We don't need to relay all our advice on Day One. Nor do we need to push our kids to make the most of every useful learning strategy. Instead, our role as parents is to provide them with opportunities to learn these strategies through interesting hobbies or goals. That way, they can test things out for themselves while steadily improving their ability to learn and grow.

Taking Action on Principle 7

Boost skill development with proven strategies. When a child commits to taking on more ambitious pursuits, they can benefit greatly from adopting proven learning methods. Here are four tips for guiding them:

1. **Encourage children to gain direct experience early and often.** Instead of getting started in an activity by developing isolated skills or knowledge, children should try to participate directly in it as early as possible. This will help them avoid the problems associated with transfer.
2. **Use purposeful practice to refine useful skills or knowledge.** There's a time and place for isolated practice. But rather than being a starting point, it should be used to address weaknesses or learning opportunities that arise through direct experience. This direct-then-drill approach helps accelerate learning.
3. **Create opportunities for rapid, relevant, and actionable feedback.** It's essential to catch mistakes and bad habits early to avoid stalled progress. Look for opportunities to have a qualified teacher, mentor, or coach evaluate your child's progress on a regular basis.
4. **Encourage a deep understanding of fundamentals.** While it's beneficial for a child to follow best practices early on, it's critical that they eventually dig deeper to understand the logic or reasoning behind these practices. That way, their knowledge will become more flexible, and they will be in a better position to adapt to unusual circumstances or novel challenges.

Remember, there is little reason to stress about what a child chooses to explore. Outside of pursuits that are truly harmful, virtually any productive pursuit will help prepare them for a brighter future. Rather than worry about interests that seem to distract from other promising pursuits, look for ways to encourage and deepen their curiosity wherever it may lead.

PRINCIPLE 8

Cultivate Happiness Through Positive Reflection

This book began with a simple premise: that one of the greatest gifts parents can give their children is an upbringing that fosters the skills, experience, and confidence needed to build a successful career.

Once again, this isn't the primary goal of being a parent or raising kids, because what we *really* want for our children is the opportunity to live a fulfilling and rewarding life, one in which they find a deep sense of purpose, build healthy relationships, and experience genuine happiness. Yet, as we also discussed in the introduction, these outcomes are far easier to achieve once someone has secured a stable, well-paying career. And this is especially true today as technological shifts, economic volatility, and political upheaval are making the world increasingly unpredictable.

That said, having a secure career is the baseline; it is necessary but not always sufficient. On its own, it doesn't automatically lead to a contented life. There are plenty of people who have achieved financial success, and even enjoy their work, yet are dissatisfied or even downright unhappy with their day-to-day existence.

The unfortunate reality is, as adults, we often find ourselves pursuing goals and dreams without pausing to enjoy the journey. And even when things are going well, there is a temptation to focus on how things could be or should be even better. We compare our lives to others, we raise the bar unrealistically on our expectations, and we obsess about our mistakes or shortcomings.

All too often, we tell ourselves we'll be happier at some point in the future. Everything will be better when we get that new car, go on a long overdue vacation, or get our kids settled into a new school. We convince ourselves that we just need to take care of a few last things and *then* we'll finally be ready to be happy. Yet, as these objectives are reached, new goals emerge to take their place, and so lasting contentment continues to be just out of reach.

But as unfortunate and common as this situation is for us adults, it may be even worse for children. Since the mid-2000s, happiness levels among U.S. adolescents have fallen off a cliff.[25] This suggests that, barring some sort of intervention, there's a good chance they will struggle even more than our generation when it comes to finding lasting joy or contentment.

The good news is that there are things we can do to better prepare them to have a more enjoyable life. Let's begin, though, by taking a moment to better understand the challenges they—and we—face.

We Aren't Wired for Lasting Contentment

The unfortunate reality is that sustained happiness isn't in human nature—quite the opposite. At the most fundamental level, we have two primary objectives in life, both of which are in conflict with lasting contentment. These include (1) our need to survive and (2) our need to pass on our genes. From a purely biological perspective, "success" in life comes down to living long enough to have one or more children.

While this is a rather cold and unemotional way of thinking about our life's purpose, understanding these two goals is critical for making sense of much of human behavior. The fact is, virtually everything we innately desire relates back to these two core objectives. The reason for this is simple: Our very existence as a species relies upon our ability to achieve these two goals, so they have played a critical role in shaping our behavior over countless generations.

The fact is, while our innate instincts are highly effective at promoting survival and reproduction, they aren't optimized for lasting contentment. Here are three examples that illustrate this conflict.

1. We Focus Excessively on Perceived Dangers, Threats, and Other Risks

Our brains are hardwired to prioritize negative information. It's why the news media is incentivized to publish stories that elicit fear or anger rather than those that convey an uplifting or positive message. And it's why, even when life is going relatively well, we tend to focus on things that might go wrong.

Our ancestors had to dwell on such things to increase their odds of survival. Anyone who happened to be born with a genetic predisposition toward being carefree was a lot less likely to be prepared for famine, drought, or an attack from a neighboring tribe or wild animal. The result is that everyone alive today is the genetic descendant of those who actively worried about potential dangers and threats—even when it wasn't strictly necessary.

The upshot is that despite the fact that we live in a world that's far, far safer than that of our ancestors, we're still wired toward this tendency. So even in the absence of major threats, we can find ourselves obsessing over relatively minor concerns. It's as if our minds constantly need something to worry about just to feel that we are remaining vigilant.

2. We Have a Strong Drive to Seek Higher Social Status

As social beings, we are constantly evaluating ourselves against others. We compare our physical appearance, intelligence, creativity, kindness, confidence, wealth, and social status day in and day out. This is so natural and automatic that we mostly do so without even being consciously aware of it. Yet, these comparisons can have a profound impact on our lives and our sense of contentment.

For example, someone who is satisfied with driving a seven-year-old car can suddenly find themselves resenting the same vehicle after a friend purchases a new car. They can feel happy about their current wardrobe up until the moment they notice most of their peers are wearing stylish new clothes. They can feel great about making $70,000 a year until they discover that several of their coworkers performing a similar job are making $90,000.

The fact is, all other things being equal, we tend to judge our lives, and the lives of others, based on social comparison rather than objective measurements of well-being. As a result, we can feel dissatisfied with our lives merely because we perceive that others are doing better than us. Again, this all relates back to our need to survive and pass on our genes—specifically, our need to climb the social ladder so we can improve our odds of attracting a mate and eventually have children.

This tendency to make social comparisons and seek increased status isn't unique to human beings. This same behavior can be seen throughout the animal kingdom, where animals sort themselves into social hierarchies based on factors such as size, strength, reproductive abilities, access to resources, and more. Higher-status animals are more likely to eat well, attract a mate, and pass on their genes.

While our human goals are more complex than animals', we're still driven by the same deep desire to gain and maintain status. This can be a good thing if it inspires us to pursue ambitious goals, strive for a better life, and make the most of the opportunities available to us. However, it can also cause us to fall into a cycle of perpetual discontentment where we're never satisfied with what we have or what we've already achieved.

It's interesting to note that constant social comparisons don't prevent us from being able to maintain healthy relationships. In fact, our ability to cooperate well with others is another key factor when it comes to improving our odds of survival and reproduction. Yet, even as we get along with those around us, we continue to compare our lives to others and look for opportunities to move up the social ladder.

3. Our Brains Reward the Pursuit of Achievement, Not Achievement Itself

One of the most fascinating discoveries about the brain has to do with motivation and the way we experience achievement. Subjectively, we tend to feel that we will be happier or more satisfied after we complete a meaningful goal, acquire something new, or reach a significant milestone. For example, we may believe we will experience a permanent increase in contentment once we secure a desirable job or purchase our first home.

However, the reality is that our brains do not reward us for achievement. Instead, they reward us for the *anticipation* of achievement. They do this by releasing dopamine, the chemical neurotransmitter that plays a critical role in our experience of pleasure and motivation. It's this brain chemical release that propels us toward new goals or pursuits by giving us the strong impression that completing them will bring an increase in pleasure or satisfaction. Yet once we reach a given objective, dopamine levels drop off, and the resulting achievement turns out to be less rewarding than the excitement we felt while closing in on it.

We've all experienced this cycle countless times, even if we weren't aware of what was really happening or why we felt the way we did after reaching a goal. For example, it's common for people to expect greater happiness after graduating from college, landing a well-paying job, finding a spouse, getting married, or purchasing their dream home. For children, an equivalent "milestone" is receiving gifts for a birthday or holiday. Whatever the specifics, our brains trick us into believing that we will experience a meaningful boost of contentment once we get what we think we want or need. Yet, time and time again, we experience only a minor bump of joy that quickly dissipates, leaving us feeling underwhelmed and eager to pursue something new.

This all makes perfect sense when we consider our core need for survival. That's because having a brain that easily settles into lasting contentment is not as useful as having one that rewards the endless pursuit of new goals or challenges. While the former may be appealing, the latter provides a strong advantage when it comes to the survival of our species, because it prevents us from growing complacent and being ill prepared for the future.

Obviously we still experience varying degrees of happiness on a regular basis. It's not as if we're completely wired to be miserable. The key point here is that our nature is designed to steer us away from *lasting* contentment. The examples provided, which show how we prioritize negative information, constantly judge ourselves relative to others, and endlessly pursue new achievements, are just three of many.

I wish I could say things are getting better, and that given all the incredible advances humans have made in medicine, science, psychology, and technology, people are happier than they've ever been. On the contrary, the opposite seems to be happening: It's becoming even more difficult for people to find joy and contentment compared to the past.

There is an effective solution to all of this—for both our children and ourselves—but before we get there, let's establish a little more context to fully appreciate the challenge we face.

The World Is Getting Better, But Happiness Is Declining

By almost any objective measure, the average person today is far better off than their ancestors. We have more stable access to food, energy, and clean water. Modern, life-saving medicines have made it far less likely that we will suffer or die from random diseases. And our daily lives have been made infinitely easier with inventions like refrigerators, dishwashers, laundry machines, the internet, search engines, chatbots, and smartphones.

And yet, again, fewer people today are satisfied with their lives compared to those living decades ago, despite enormous advances in medicine and technology. Perhaps unsurprisingly, this has led many people to long for a return to a simpler, supposedly better time. On one hand, it can be tempting to assume such people have an overly romanticized view of the past, one that fails to appreciate the remarkable progress that has been made in recent decades. On the other hand, it's also true that not all "progress" has been positive for society.

Consider the following three developments that have aggravated our natural tendencies.

DINNER TIME CONVERSATIONS

1. Increased Exposure to Negative Information

Our access to information has grown exponentially over the past few decades. It wasn't long ago that the volume of news we consumed was tightly constrained by the space available in local newspapers or the time allotted to nightly news broadcasts. But, with the shift to online news and the proliferation of modern smartphones, we now have virtually unlimited access to real-time information from around the world.

The result is that we are now inundated with news that often plays into our natural tendency to focus on dangers, fears, and other potential threats. And, to make matters worse, media producers (traditional news outlets and also bloggers, streamers, YouTubers, podcasters, and the like) have an incredibly strong incentive to publish stories that are designed to stir up negative emotions, such as anger and outrage. Not only are these kinds of stories more likely to draw our attention, but they're also more likely to spread on social media platforms that amplify attention-grabbing content.

To an extent, we obviously have the option to go out of our way to avoid negative news and social media. But emotionally charged stories are so pervasive today that we can be exposed to them at pretty much any moment, whether through casual conversations with coworkers, friends, or family or even a TV blaring at the airport. The result is that we are much more likely to find ourselves feeling disempowered, angry, or outraged than we might have in past years.

2. Far More Opportunities for Social Comparison

As the world has become increasingly connected, we've also experienced a sharp increase in opportunities to compare ourselves to others. Not long ago, people primarily measured their skills and achievements against those in their immediate social circle or local community. More often than not, these sorts of comparisons took place between people with similar opportunities when it comes to education, social connections, and career options.

Today, social media platforms have turned social comparison into a global competition. It's now easier than ever to compare ourselves against the most accomplished people in any given dimension of life. No matter our life circumstances, we can always find someone who appears to be richer, smarter, more successful, or happier than us. Often, these comparisons are highly inaccurate, because people are far more likely to share their greatest hits while keeping their doubts, fears, and shortcomings to themselves. (Not to mention that many of the sharers are intentionally misrepresenting their lives.)

This explosion of (over)sharing has led to greater dissatisfaction for *everyone* who participates in it. That's because, once again, we judge ourselves and our lives based on social comparison rather than objective measurements of well-being. Teddy Roosevelt had it right with his famous quip that "Comparison is the thief of joy." The moment we compare our achievements to someone more successful than us, we reduce any feelings of satisfaction that we might otherwise enjoy. Thus social media, and the internet more broadly, makes it more likely that people will find themselves dissatisfied with their lives.

3. An Explosion of Attractive Opportunities

Compared to our ancestors, we have so many more options available to us today. We have a greater choice of potential hobbies, careers, schools, colleges, entertainment, and even relationships. On one hand, this is great because it means we're able to select things that are more closely aligned with our needs and preferences. On the other hand, studies have consistently shown that we can end up less satisfied with our choices when we're forced to select one option from many promising alternatives. The psychologist Barry Schwartz makes this case in his 2004 bestseller *The Paradox of Choice*. He writes, "Learning to choose is hard. Learning to choose well is harder. And learning to choose well in a world of unlimited possibilities is harder still, perhaps too hard."[26]

Much of this comes down to the sense of loss that takes place when we make a final choice. For example, a student who commits to pursuing an economics degree does so knowing they are sacrificing other options, such as a degree in computer science, psychology, or philosophy. In these kinds of situations, where a choice involves rejecting viable alternatives, we have a tendency to dwell on what is being lost rather than what is being gained.

This dynamic can contribute to the cycle of discontentment because, as explained earlier, our brains reward the *anticipation* of achievement rather than achievement itself. So if a student pursuing an economics degree believes they will receive a lasting boost of contentment after graduation but that satisfaction quickly dissipates, they may end up second-guessing their choice, believing they would have been more satisfied had they chosen differently.

This pattern can play out in all kinds of decisions, including ones relating to your career, vehicle, home, hobbies, vacations, and romantic relationships. In an age of exponentially increased options, it's no wonder that many people find themselves less satisfied with their choices. No matter how many interesting experiences they have or goals they achieve, they may still feel like they are missing out.

The Solution Is Right in Front of Us—
If We're Willing to See It

So much of our feeling of discontent stems from taking things for granted. We rarely think about our health until it's at risk. We often fail to appreciate key relationships until they break down or we lose someone close to us. And we don't always realize how much fulfillment or meaning we're getting from a hobby or a career until something prevents us from participating in it. In short, we often fail to appreciate many of the best things in life because we're distracted by negative information, social comparison, and the pursuit of further achievement.

This doesn't mean we should stop striving for more. Nor does it mean we should accept complacency. Instead, we must strike a healthier balance between seeking more and appreciating the things we already have. Rather than putting our happiness on pause until we reach some future goal or milestone, we must focus on enjoying the journey itself—and, in the process, help our children do the same.

A simple but powerful way to accomplish this is to make an effort to focus on the rewarding aspects of our lives. We can do this by developing a habit of positive reflection, one that allows us to take note of the many things we are grateful for, such as continued health, rewarding relationships, or the opportunity to engage in a meaningful hobby or project.

Religions have long understood the importance of gratitude and positive reflection, and they've established rituals and belief systems around giving thanks and celebrating meaningful milestones. Perhaps the most recognizable example of this is the practice of daily prayer, when time is often set aside to give thanks for things that are going well.

Unfortunately, these kinds of rituals have been in decline in recent years. Today, fewer families sit down for shared meals, engage in meaningful conversations, or set aside time for positive reflection. As a result, many children are growing up without the tools and support that could make it easier for them to live a happier life, regardless of the challenges they face.

Build a Simple Habit of Positive Reflection

I happened to be raised in a family that practiced prayer before every family meal. Immediately upon sitting down to eat, we would go around the table and take turns sharing things we were grateful for. Then, one of us would be invited to say a prayer on behalf of the family that summarized many of the things that had been shared. Only after the prayer was complete would the meal begin.

I didn't realize the positive impact of this simple daily habit until many years later. In fact, I didn't give it much thought at all; it was just something we did before family meals, like setting the table. But in recent years, as I've learned more about the value of positive reflection, I've realized the valuable role this routine played in directing our attention toward rewarding, satisfying, or otherwise positive elements of life. And how it helped us mitigate our default tendencies to focus primarily on our fears, worries, or concerns.

You don't have to be religious to benefit from positive reflection. The essential task is simply setting aside a few moments each day to identify and celebrate the things you're grateful for. Again, this can include simple things, like rewarding relationships, engaging hobbies or projects, or anything else that might otherwise be taken for granted. Through this process we can find greater satisfaction in everyday life, even as we continue to face new challenges. Indeed, a strong sense of gratitude can help us navigate setbacks with greater ease.

The real magic happens when this routine continues over many days. As family members run out of the obvious things to share—say, being grateful for a best friend or favorite hobby—they begin to notice and appreciate smaller details of life, knowing they'll be asked to share something new at the next meal. As a result, this simple practice rewires their brain to actively focus on the many positives that already exist in their world, things they simply hadn't noticed before. The effect can be life-altering.

As an added benefit, this practice is also a powerful way to prepare for meaningful conversations. On any given day, children may arrive at the dinner table with a bad attitude or a negative mindset. They may be dealing with strong emotions or difficult challenges or simply feel tired and disengaged. But by beginning each meal with a moment of positive reflection, we can help them overcome their negativity and maybe even get a fresh jolt of positive energy, one that makes it much more likely that they will engage in the conversations that follow.

Perhaps most important of all, this practice can transform how our children feel about themselves, see the rest of the world, and relate to other people. Our kids are more likely to pursue ambitious goals when they're able to recognize and appreciate small wins. They are more likely to overcome obstacles when they routinely focus on the progress they've made rather than just dwelling on the difficult road ahead. And they're more likely to connect and work well with others when they develop and maintain a more optimistic, grateful disposition.

The benefits are just as significant for us as parents, of course. By practicing gratitude and celebrating small wins, it's easier to stay calm during challenging times. It can also help us avoid getting stuck in negative emotions that can prevent us from finding joy and satisfaction in life.

Balance Is Essential

Striving for positivity isn't always healthy. Sometimes people focus excessively on the good things in life as a way to mask or run from genuine problems. They celebrate positive experiences only to ignore or downplay critical unresolved issues. As a result, their problems fester and grow until they can no longer be ignored, at which point things are often far worse than they could have been.

Practicing gratitude isn't about ignoring life's challenges. Rather, it's about helping children maintain a balanced outlook—keeping the positives in view as they work through the negatives. By embracing this mindset, they can appreciate their accomplishments while still pursuing new goals, even if some of those efforts fail. It's a way to counteract the natural human tendencies that might otherwise stop them from fully enjoying life.

How to Build a Habit of Positive Reflection

A great way to begin is to start small and lead by example. Rather than making a big show of kicking off a new family routine, simply explain to your children before dinner that you'd love to hear about what they're enjoying in life. Then give everyone a chance to mention something they're thankful for, a recent success, or a highlight from their day.

You can set the tone by first sharing your own response. I recommend using a simple pattern that's easy to repeat, such as "I'm grateful for X, because Y" or "I'm proud of finishing X, because Y." It's best to coordinate with any other adults who will be present ahead of time to ensure they're on board and prepared to share a response after you. That way your children get further examples of how they're expected to participate and a few extra moments to come up with their own answer.

Once everyone has had a chance to share something, quickly recap some of the things that were mentioned. Later, as the routine becomes more ingrained, you can select a random family member to do this last part. Just like my family's practice of dinnertime prayer, the purpose here is to both reinforce the positive things that were shared while also encouraging everyone to listen carefully (as they should, since they may be called upon to provide the closing recap!).

Some children may struggle to come up with an initial response, and that's okay. When that happens, you can simply let them know they can think about it for a day and present their answer at the next meal. Before that meal begins, give them a quick reminder to be sure they lock in their answer. That way they won't get caught off guard a second time or make a habit of not having a ready answer.

When a child provides a unique or interesting response, consider reinforcing it with descriptive praise. Instead of defaulting to generic comments like, "Thank you for sharing" or "That's great," point out what you specifically appreciate about their answer. For instance, if they express gratitude for something most people overlook, you might say, "I love how you highlighted something we usually take for granted!" Likewise, if they mention a small victory on the path to a bigger goal, you could respond, "Yes, every step counts. I'm glad you're noticing your progress!"

Just remember to avoid offering fake or preemptive praise. As you may recall from principle 6, it's easy to make the mistake of using praise to encourage behaviors that haven't yet materialized. For example, a parent might make the mistake of saying, "I like how you always come up with thoughtful responses," even when a child is failing to do so. Again, praise is most effective as a tool for *reinforcing* existing behavior, so it's best to hold off on using it until it's truly appropriate.

Once all your children are comfortable with this routine, you can start to encourage multiple responses. A great way to do this is to once again lead by example—in this case by saying something like, "I'm thankful for a few things today..." and then sharing two or three examples. That way, you'll subtly convey that it's okay for them to have more than one response without setting a firm expectation that they must do so.

Of course, if your family happens to practice daily prayer, or a similar religious ritual, you can simply build on that foundation instead of creating an entirely new routine.

Taking Action on Principle 8

Cultivate happiness through positive reflection. A daily gratitude routine gives everyone in the family a chance to push back against the natural tendency to dwell on negative information, social comparisons, and other challenges in life. Here are five tips to get started:

1. **Begin with a small request.** Avoid introducing this practice with a lengthy explanation of its benefits. Instead, simply express how you'd love to hear more about what everyone is enjoying or appreciating in life. Then, ask each person to share something they're grateful for, a small win they recently experienced, or anything else they enjoyed about their day.
2. **Lead by example to set the tone.** Use a simple pattern such as, "I'm grateful for X, because Y." If other adults will be present, coordinate with them in advance to ensure they're ready to provide an answer after you. That way children have an extra opportunity to see what's expected of them.
3. **Invite children to participate.** Start with a child who is likely to have an answer ready (i.e., someone who recently accomplished a milestone or expressed gratitude in a different setting). A great response from them can help set the tone.

4. **If a child isn't ready to answer, that's okay.** Let them know they can respond at the next dinner. Then, give them a quick reminder the next day to ensure they have an answer prepared.
5. **Reinforce great responses with detailed praise.** Describe exactly what you liked most about their answer. Was it thoughtful or original? Did it highlight something that is often taken for granted? Let them know.

You don't have to get this perfect on the first try. As always, the beauty of having a daily routine is that you can make small changes from day-to-day until you find the most effective approach. Focus on leading by example, listening carefully to your children's responses, and showing that you appreciate their participation. This simple routine can have a profound impact on your family's happiness and contentment.

Now it's time for a quick recap of everything we've covered (and a few closing thoughts).

Conclusion

We started this book by highlighting how unpredictable the world has become. Society has changed dramatically over the past few decades, and the pace of change is only accelerating. Because of advancements in automation, AI, and other disruptive technologies, it's no longer possible to predict what the future holds for our kids, particularly when it comes to their careers. And yet, as parents, we still want to do everything we can to set them up for success.

Setting them up, however, does not—and cannot—mean clearing a path for them or jumping in to solve things on their behalf. The solution laid out in this book is to raise kids to become *curious problem solvers* who are eager to take on new challenges and take pride in their ability to adapt to sudden changes. To that end, our core mission is to provide them with opportunities to nurture their natural curiosity, gain diverse life experience, and discover their capacity to overcome difficult challenges. In doing so, we help them develop the genuine confidence needed to thrive, regardless of whatever surprises the future has in store. Only then will they be able to take advantage of opportunities that come their way and enjoy a life of security and, hopefully, happiness.

Over the course of this book, we explored eight principles that can help them build a successful life and career. Before we part ways, let's quickly review the most essential information.

Everything Begins with Nurturing Meaningful Relationships

The most critical step we can take is to build a daily habit of having casual yet meaningful conversations with our children (principle 1). This routine is the foundation on which all further progress is built. It's what puts us in a position to truly understand what our children are going through so we can more effectively support their growth and development.

Creating this habit begins with selecting a consistent time and place to engage in it. For many families, dinner time will be the most convenient and consistent opportunity to have a meaningful conversation. However, if that doesn't work for your family, other times of the day can work, too. The most important thing is for the routine to be consistent, so it can become an automatic habit.

It's also useful to decide on a specific cue or trigger that indicates it's time for the routine to begin. For example, when someone calls out "dinner time" to bring the family together, this simple phrase can also serve as a cue that it's time for the routine to start. After hearing these words, take a moment to let go of any distractions so you can be fully present during the meal. That way, when you sit down with your kids, you're ready to focus your attention on them.

This daily routine is obviously *not* the only opportunity or responsibility we have as parents. Making the most of this time is no substitute for being present in other key moments. Rather, this routine serves as a foundation for creating further connections.

Use the Remaining Principles to Support Your Children's Growth

Once you've established your daily routine, you'll be in a far stronger position to apply the other seven principles to further support your

CONCLUSION

children's growth and development. Here's a quick recap of them (including the all-important first principle):

1. Support kids' growth with a daily routine.
2. Nurture kids' curiosity through self-selected hobbies.
3. Build flexible knowledge through diverse experience.
4. Shape positive behaviors with effective modeling.
5. Nurture problem solving with open-ended questions.
6. Reinforce kids' growth with detailed praise.
7. Boost skill development with proven strategies.
8. Cultivate happiness through positive reflection.

The chapters exploring each principle contain a wealth of valuable insights and tips that you'll want to review from time to time. I recommend revisiting them even if you think you don't need to; chances are high that you'll see some useful bits of information you forgot about.

To help make this process even easier, I've created a bonus resource you can use anytime you need a quick refresher. It's a printable one-page cheat sheet that can be mounted on the inside of a kitchen cabinet or pantry door so you can quickly revisit any of the principles before, during, or after a family meal.

You can download your free one-page cheat sheet at DinnerTimeConversations.com/cheatsheet.

Establish a Family Culture Where Success Is Inevitable

The true value of the approach outlined in this book will be unlocked when these principles become a normal, automatic part of your daily life. As family members fall in love with pursuing various interests, taking on difficult challenges, and celebrating small wins, progress becomes all but inevitable.

Establishing these habits is crucial to building a family culture of success and gratitude. Rather than just telling kids that they have the potential to achieve anything in life, we must help them get a taste of their potential firsthand. Not just once or twice, but as a normal part of their ongoing lives. This is the key to raising kids that become truly confident in their ability to take on life's challenges.

With all that said, I want to remind you that you do *not* need to be perfect as a parent. No one conversation is going to make or break the future success of your children. If things occasionally go off the rails, or you forget to make use of a helpful tool or insight, that's completely okay. What matters most is that you build steady momentum by engaging in casual yet meaningful conversations every day. Doing so will create endless opportunities to understand their interests, ask great questions, and support their growth.

Build a Community of Like-Minded Parents

Obviously, we are not the only adults who will influence our children's development. Many other adults will play a critical role in their lives, including grandparents, aunts, uncles, teachers, coaches, and parents of their friends. While these individuals will hopefully play a positive role, their approaches to building life skills may unintentionally undermine or conflict with some of our own efforts.

On one hand, this isn't necessarily a bad thing. I tend to believe that so long as people are well intentioned and doing their best, it's generally healthy for children to be exposed to a variety of parenting or mentoring styles, even if they occasionally conflict with our own. Not to mention, keeping our children isolated from the outside world is both impractical and goes against the core principles of this book. On the other hand, it can be beneficial if some of the key influences in our children's lives follow a similar approach to us.

Accordingly, if you agree with the principles in this book, I encourage you to share and discuss them with close friends and members of your extended family. If you have a physical copy of the book, consider lending it to them so they will be in a better position to support the growth of your children. As a potential bonus, when you share the recommendations in this book with other parents, you create an opportunity for them to consider taking a similar approach when raising their own children.

I truly believe one of the best ways to build a stronger future for *everyone* is to raise a generation of kids who are more capable, confident, and adaptable in the face of change. This is not a competition in which other kids must lose or fall behind for ours to succeed. Everyone is better off living in a world where the next generation is able to find purpose in solving difficult problems, creating innovative solutions, and living more rewarding and fulfilling lives.

Here's How to Take Action Today

1. **Identify the time and place for your family routine.** I recommend that you strongly consider family dinner first, but if that doesn't work, review the tips in principle 1 to find a good alternative. The key is to find a time and place that is available on a daily basis.
2. **Download the free one-page cheat sheet.** This will provide a quick and convenient way to review all eight principles. I recommend you print it out and mount it on the inside of a kitchen cabinet door (or anywhere that's easy to access), so it can be quickly reviewed anytime. Download it at DinnerTimeConversations.com/cheatsheet.

3. **Think of the names of 2–3 adults who influence your kids.** Are there neighbors, aunts, uncles, teachers, or family friends who play a key role in their lives? Consider lending them a copy of this book so you can nurture a community of like-minded parents.

That's it! Go download the cheat sheet and get started.

Acknowledgments

This book came together slowly over five years, and it simply wouldn't exist without the influence, support, and encouragement of so many people.

First, I want to thank my parents and grandparents. They shaped not only the way I was raised but also how I approached the ideas explored throughout this book. My father, Howard Kettner, in particular, had an outsized impact—sharing thoughtful feedback and helpful insights throughout the writing process.

I'm also incredibly grateful to the many people who took time to share their perspectives in early interviews or gave feedback on early drafts. This includes my mother, Tina; my wife, Gabriela; my brothers, Michael, Chad, and Jordan; and my sisters-in-law, Heidi, Rachel, and Rachelle; as well as Kyle, Elger, Jame, Sean, and Jeff. Their input helped make this book much stronger and clearer than it would have been otherwise.

Along the way, I was deeply inspired by the work of countless authors and researchers—many of whom are referenced in these pages. Their insights helped clarify, support, and deepen the principles we covered.

Parts of the book were also inspired by my journey as an entrepreneur. In that regard, I've been fortunate to learn a lot from my father; my business partner, Jared Falk; and the many amazing people I've had the opportunity to work with at Musora, Drumeo, Pianote, and Guitareo.

DINNER TIME CONVERSATIONS

The spark for this book came from Rob Fitzpatrick, whose book *Write Useful Books* helped me see that a project like this was not only possible but worth pursuing. Charlie Holiday played a key role in helping me stick with the writing process over many, many months. And I'm especially thankful to Adam Rosen, my developmental editor, whose guidance was instrumental in refining the structure and flow of the final manuscript.

Last but not least, I want to thank my wife and three boys. They are the inspiration for researching and writing about *this* specific topic.

Notes

1. TED, "The riddle of experience vs. memory | Daniel Kahneman," posted March 1, 2010, YouTube video, 18:07 to 18:13, https://www.youtube.com/watch?v=XgRlrBl-7Yg&t=1087s.
2. Bureau of Labor Statistics, U.S. Department of Labor, "Number of Jobs, Labor Market Experience, Marital Status, and Health for Those Born 1957-1964," news release, August 22, 2023, https://www.bls.gov/news.release/pdf/nlsoy.pdf.
3. Diego Ardila et al., "End-to-End Lung Cancer Screening with Three-Dimensional Deep Learning on Low-Dose Chest Computed Tomography," *Nature Medicine* 25, no. 6 (May 20, 2019): 954–961, https://doi.org/10.1038/s41591-019-0447-x.
4. *2024 Gen Z and Millennial Survey: Living and working with purpose in a transforming world* (Deloitte), May 2024, https://www.deloitte.com/content/dam/assets-shared/docs/campaigns/2024/deloitte-2024-genz-millennial-survey.pdf?dlva=3; Naina Dhingra et al., "Help Your Employees Find Purpose—or Watch Them Leave," McKinsey & Company, accessed February 12, 2025, https://www.mckinsey.com/capabilities/people-and-organizational-performance/our-insights/help-your-employees-find-purpose-or-watch-them-leave.
5. James Clear, *Atomic Habits* (Avery, 2018), 27.
6. "Weighing the Benefits and Costs of Extracurriculars," SSM Health Cardinal Glennon Children's Hospital, accessed February 12, 2025, https://www.ssmhealth.com/newsroom/blogs/ssm-health-matters/april-2023/weighing-the-benefits-and-costs-of-extracurriculars.

7 Nicole B. Perry et al., "Childhood Self-Regulation as a Mechanism Through Which Early Overcontrolling Parenting Is Associated with Adjustment in Preadolescence," *Developmental Psychology* 54, no. 8 (2018): 1542–1554, https://pubmed.ncbi.nlm.nihgov/29911876/.

8 Jenny Anderson and Rebecca Winthrop, "Giving Kids Some Autonomy Has Surprising Results," *New York Times*, January 2, 2025, https://www.nytimes.com/2025/01/02/opinion/children-choices-goal-setting.html.

9 David Epstein, *Range: Why Generalists Triumph in a Specialized World* (Penguin, 2019), 76.

10 Robin M. Hogarth et al., "The Two Settings of Kind and Wicked Learning Environments," *Current Directions in Psychological Science* 24, no. 5 (2015): 379–385, http://www.jstor.org/stable/44318900.

11 Lewis Thomas, *The Youngest Science: Notes of a Medicine Watcher* (Bantam Books, 1983), 20.

12 David Guest, "Managers in focus as the skills gap closes," *Independent* (London), September 17, 1991.

13 Scott Adams, "The Kristina Talent Stack," *Scott Adams's Blog*, December 27, 2016, archived June 4, 2024, at https://web.archive.org/web/20170604015221/http://blog.dilbert.com/post/155029617616/the-kristina-talent-stack.

14 Peter Gray, "Unsolicited Advice: I Hate It, You Hate It; So Do Your Kids," *Psychology Today*, December 22, 2010, https://www.psychologytoday.com/us/blog/freedom-to-learn/201012/unsolicited-advice-i-hate-it-you-hate-it-so-do-your-kids.

15 Carol Dweck, *Mindset: The New Psychology of Success* (Random House, 2006), 9.

16 Anders Ericsson and Robert Pool, *Peak: Secrets from the New Science of Expertise* (HarperCollins, 2016), chap. 8, Kindle.

17 Ericsson and Pool, *Peak*, chap. 1, Kindle.

18 Dweck, *Mindset*, 178.

19 Scott H. Young, *Ultralearning: Master Hard Skills, Outsmart the Competition, and Accelerate Your Career* (HarperCollins, 2019), 90.

20 Young, *Ultralearning*, 99.

21 Ericsson and Pool, *Peak*, chap. 1, Kindle.

22 Ericsson and Pool, *Peak*, chap. 6, Kindle.

23 Young, *Ultralearning*, 150.
24 Jeffrey D. Karpicke and Janell R. Blunt, "Retrieval Practice Produces More Learning Than Elaborative Studying with Concept Mapping," *Science* 331, no. 6018 (2011): 772–775, https://doi.org/10.1126/science.1199327.
25 Jean M. Twenge, "The Sad State of Happiness in the United States and the Role of Digital Media," in *World Happiness Report 2019*, ed. John F. Helliwell, Richard Layard, and Jeffrey D. Sachs (Gallup, Oxford Wellbeing Research Centre, UN Sustainable Development Solutions Network, and WHR Editorial Board, 2019), chap. 5, https://worldhappiness.report/ed/2019/the-sad-state-of-happiness-in-the-united-states-and-the-role-of-digital-media/.
26 Barry Schwartz, *The Paradox of Choice: Why More Is Less, Revised Edition* (Ecco, 2016), 148.

Works Cited

Adams, Scott. "The Kristina Talent Stack." *Scott Adams's Blog*, December 27, 2016. Archived June 4, 2024. https://web.archive.org/web/20170604015221/http://blog.dilbert.com/post/155029617616/the-kristina-talent-stack.

Anderson, Jenny, and Rebecca Winthrop. "Giving Kids Some Autonomy Has Surprising Results." *New York Times*, January 2, 2025. https://www.nytimes.com/2025/01/02/opinion/children-choices-goal-setting.html.

Ardila, Diego, et al. "End-to-End Lung Cancer Screening with Three-Dimensional Deep Learning on Low-Dose Chest Computed Tomography." *Nature Medicine 25*, no. 6 (May 20, 2019): 954–961. https://doi.org/10.1038/s41591-019-0447-x.

Bureau of Labor Statistics, U.S. Department of Labor. "Number of Jobs, Labor Market Experience, Marital Status, and Health for Those Born 1957–1964." News release, August 22, 2023. https://www.bls.gov/news.release/pdf/nlsoy.pdf.

Clear, James. *Atomic Habits*. New York: Avery, 2018.

2024 Gen Z and Millennial Survey: Living and Working with Purpose in a Transforming World. *Deloitte*, May 2024. https://www.deloitte.com/content/dam/assets-shared/docs/campaigns/2024/deloitte-2024-genz-millennial-survey.pdf?dlva=3.

Dhingra, Naina, Jonathan Emmett, Andrew Samo, and Bill Schaninger. "Help Your Employees Find Purpose—or Watch Them Leave." McKinsey

& Company. Accessed February 12, 2025. https://www.mckinsey.com/capabilities/people-and-organizational-performance/our-insights/help-your-employees-find-purpose-or-watch-them-leave.

Dweck, Carol. *Mindset: The New Psychology of Success*. New York: Random House, 2006.

Epstein, David. *Range: Why Generalists Triumph in a Specialized World*. New York: Penguin, 2019.

Ericsson, Anders, and Robert Pool. *Peak: Secrets from the New Science of Expertise*. New York: HarperCollins, 2016. Kindle edition.

Gray, Peter. "Unsolicited Advice: I Hate It, You Hate It; So Do Your Kids." *Psychology Today*, December 22, 2010. https://www.psychologytoday.com/us/blog/freedom-to-learn/201012/unsolicited-advice-i-hate-it-you-hate-it-so-do-your-kids.

Guest, David. "Managers in Focus as the Skills Gap Closes." *Independent* (London), September 17, 1991.

Hogarth, Robin M., Emre Soyer, and Anuj K. Shah. "The Two Settings of Kind and Wicked Learning Environments." *Current Directions in Psychological Science 24*, no. 5 (2015): 379–385. http://www.jstor.org/stable/44318900.

Kahneman, Daniel. "The Riddle of Experience vs. Memory." *TED*. YouTube video, 18:07–18:13. Posted March 1, 2010. https://www.youtube.com/watch?v=XgRlrBl-7Yg&t=1087s.

Karpicke, Jeffrey D., and Janell R. Blunt. "Retrieval Practice Produces More Learning Than Elaborative Studying with Concept Mapping." *Science 331*, no. 6018 (2011): 772–775. https://doi.org/10.1126/science.1199327.

Perry, Nicole B., et al. "Childhood Self-Regulation as a Mechanism Through Which Early Overcontrolling Parenting Is Associated with Adjustment in Preadolescence." *Developmental Psychology 54*, no. 8 (August 2018): 1542–1554. https://pubmed.ncbi.nlm.nih.gov/29911876/.

Schwartz, Barry. *The Paradox of Choice: Why More Is Less.* Revised ed. New York: Ecco, 2016.

SSM Health Cardinal Glennon Children's Hospital. "Weighing the Benefits and Costs of Extracurriculars." Accessed February 12, 2025. https://www.ssmhealth.com/newsroom/blogs/ssm-health-matters/april-2023/weighing-the-benefits-and-costs-of-extracurriculars.

Thomas, Lewis. *The Youngest Science: Notes of a Medicine Watcher.* New York: Bantam Books, 1983.

Twenge, Jean M. "The Sad State of Happiness in the United States and the Role of Digital Media." In *World Happiness Report 2019*, edited by John F. Helliwell, Richard Layard, and Jeffrey D. Sachs, chap. 5. Gallup, Oxford Wellbeing Research Centre, UN Sustainable Development Solutions Network, and WHR Editorial Board, 2019. https://worldhappiness.report/ed/2019/the-sad-state-of-happiness-in-the-united-states-and-the-role-of-digital-media/.

Young, Scott H. *Ultralearning: Master Hard Skills, Outsmart the Competition, and Accelerate Your Career.* New York: HarperCollins, 2019.

www.ingramcontent.com/pod-product-compliance
Lightning Source LLC
Chambersburg PA
CBHW071208070526
44584CB00019B/2956